Collins | English for Exams

Cambridge English Qualifications

Activities for A2 Key for Schools

Published by Collins
An imprint of HarperCollins Publishers
1 Robroyston Gate,
Glasgow
G33 1JN

HarperCollins Publishers
Macken House
39/40 Mayor Street Upper
Dublin 1
D01 C9W8
Ireland

First edition 2021

10 9 8 7 6 5

© HarperCollins Publishers 2021

ISBN 978-0-00-846116-4

Collins® is a registered trademark of
HarperCollins Publishers Limited

collins.co.uk/elt

A catalogue record for this book is available from
the British Library.

Author: Rebecca Adlard
Series editor: Celia Wigley
For the Publisher: Gillian Bowman and Kerry Ferguson
Typesetter: Davidson Publishing Solutions
Artwork: Aptara (pages 61 and 77) and Q2A Media
(pages 81 and 83)
Audio recorded and produced by Tom Ottway,
Language Umbrella Media
Cover illustration © Maria Herbert-Liew 2021

Printed and bound in the UK by Ashford Colour Ltd.

The Publishers gratefully acknowledge the permission
granted to reproduce the copyright material in this
book. Whilst every effort has been made to trace
the copyright holders, in cases where this has been
unsuccessful, or if any have inadvertently been
overlooked, the Publishers would gladly receive any
information enabling them to rectify any error or
omission at the first opportunity.

All exam-style questions and sample answers in
this title were written by the author.

About the author

Rebecca Adlard is an experienced ELT professional
specialising in very young and young learners. She has
over 20 years' ELT experience and has taught English
and worked on various language projects in the UK,
Sweden, Denmark, Australia, Syria, China and Spain.
She is co-director of Language Umbrella Ltd.

Acknowledgements

We would like to thank those authors and publishers who
kindly gave permission for copyright material to be used in
the Collins Corpus. We would also like to thank Times
Newspapers Ltd for providing valuable data.

Photo credits

Shutterstock: p22 crossword clue 3 down (Goncalo_
Castelo_Soares), p40 (Anton_Ivanov), p46 vocabulary
exercise 1, photo 1 (Duncan Cuthbertson), p46
vocabulary exercise 1, photo 6 (Leigh Trail), p50
clue 2 (Hadrian), p63 vocabulary exercise 3, photo 4
(Jack Cousin). All other images from Shutterstock

MIX
Paper | Supporting
responsible forestry
FSC™ C007454

This book contains FSC™ certified paper and other controlled
sources to ensure responsible forest management.

For more information visit: www.harpercollins.co.uk/green

Dear Student

Welcome to Collins Activities for A2 Key for Schools!

Here's some information on how to use this book so that you get the most out of your studies.

This book has 20 units and each unit covers a different topic. The topics and vocabulary in this book are from the official 2020 Cambridge A2 Key for Schools Vocabulary List. This means that the words you are learning will help you do well in the Cambridge A2 Key for Schools exam. You can do the units in any order you choose.

Each unit has activities that practise the four skills that are in the test: reading, writing, listening and speaking. There are also fun activities practising vocabulary, spelling and grammar.

The reading, writing, listening and speaking activities are similar to those in the exam. Next to each activity, you'll see a note to say which part of the official Cambridge A2 Key for Schools test the activity is practising. For example, if you are doing a Reading activity and you see **PART 1** , this means the activity is preparation for Reading Part 1 of the test.

There is audio for the listening and speaking activities, which will also help your pronunciation. If you see this icon 🎧, please listen to the audio, which you can find online at **collins.co.uk/eltresources**. The track number is under the icon. In the listening part of the exam, the audio is played twice. So I suggest you play the audio for the listening activities twice.

If you see this icon ✋, this is a helping hand. It means that the information here can help you improve your English or do better in the exam.

At the front of the book, you will find a table showing you what's in every unit. At the back of the book, you will find the answers, the audio scripts and word lists for every unit.

I hope you enjoy using this book. Good luck with your studies!

Rebecca Adlard

(the author)

contents

Vocabulary

1 Complete the words.

1

b _ _ t

2

e _ _ _ i n _ s

3

b _ _ c _ l _ _

4

g _ _ _ e s

5

_ _ o _ s _

6

_ _ b _ e _ _ a

2 Look at the photo of the woman and read the words. Which things *isn't* she wearing?

1 sweater ☐

2 T-shirt ☐

3 trainers ☐

4 boots ☐

5 sunglasses ☐

6 tie ☐

7 scarf ☐

8 hat ☐

9 raincoat ☐

10 skirt ☐

3 Read the description and match to the correct photo A or B.

James is in the park. He's wearing jeans and trainers today. He's not wearing a jumper because it's sunny and warm. He's wearing a T-shirt. He isn't wearing a shirt. But he is wearing a cap.

A

☐

B

☐

Grammar: **Present continuous: to talk about what is happening now**

He's *wearing* jeans and trainers today.

Write a sentence using the present continuous to describe what the boy is and isn't wearing in the **other** photo in Activity 3.

Speaking

PART 1

 Listen and answer the questions about clothes and accessories.

1

> **Speaking tip**
>
> Use adjectives to make your answers more interesting.
>
> What clothes and accessories are you wearing now?
>
> *I'm wearing a soft blue jumper, a black skirt and some small purple earrings.*

1   What clothes and accessories are you wearing now?

2   What clothes do you wear to school? Do you have to wear a school uniform?

3   What type of clothes do you not like wearing?

4   What do you like wearing in hot weather?

5   Do you ever wear any jewellery?

Reading

Read the text about school uniform. For each question, choose the correct answer A, B or C.

My new school uniform
By Helena Hodges, age 10

I've just started at a new school and it is quite different to my old school. In my old school we didn't have to wear a school uniform, so I wore all my favourite clothes. I usually wore jeans and a T-shirt or jumper. And in the summer when it was hot, I wore shorts or a skirt.

In my new school we have to wear a school uniform. Our school uniform is green – I hate green! My favourite colour is purple. I have to wear a green skirt, green tights or long socks, a white blouse and a green jacket. And the worst thing is we have to wear a tie too! It's not very comfortable. I love wearing trainers, but in my new school I have to wear shoes – even in winter! And I really don't like looking the same as everyone else in the school.

1 **What is different about Helena's new school?**

   A   She has to wear a uniform.

   B   She doesn't have to wear a uniform.

   C   It's a lot bigger than her old school.

2 **How does Helena feel about wearing a school uniform?**

   A   She likes it because it's her favourite colour.

   B   She thinks it isn't very comfortable.

   C   She likes looking the same as the other students.

3 **What doesn't Helena like wearing in the winter?**

   A   trainers

   B   a skirt

   C   shoes

Listening

For each question, choose the correct picture A, B or C.

Listening tip For Listening Part 1, read the questions and look at all three of the possible answers before you listen to the audio.

1 What is Grace wearing to the party this evening?

A   B   C

2 How much does the red jacket cost?

£ 14.50	£ 12	£ 20
A	B	C

Grammar: **Present continuous: to talk about future plans**

What *is* Grace *wearing* to the party this evening?

Write a sentence using present continuous to describe things you are doing this weekend.

Writing

Write an email.

Your friend is having a party this weekend. They want to invite the English student in your class, Freddy, but they don't speak English very well. Write a text message in English to Freddy.

Say:

- he's invited to a party and whose party it is
- when and where it is
- what you're wearing to the party and ask him what he is wearing.

Write **25 words** or more.

Vocabulary

1 **Listen and write the words in the correct places.**

1 _____ 2 _____ 3 _____

4 _____

5 _____

6 _____

9 _____ 8 _____ 7 _____

2 **Look at the photo. Tick the things you can see.**

bottle ☐   bowl ☐   cup ☐   fork ☐   glass ☐   knife ☐

menu ☐   plate ☐   sauce ☐   spoon ☐

3 Match the words with their definitions.

> barbecue breakfast café chef dinner fridge
> kitchen lunch picnic snack

1 _____: a simple meal that is quick to prepare and to eat

2 _____: a cook in a restaurant

3 _____: a meal that you cook and eat outside

4 _____: a piece of equipment that is cold inside – you keep food and drink in it

5 _____: the first meal of the day

6 _____: a meal you eat outdoors – usually in a park or a forest, or at the beach

7 _____: the main meal of the day – usually in the evening

8 _____: a room that is used for cooking

9 _____: the meal that you have in the middle of the day

10 _____: a place where you can buy drinks and small meals

Speaking

 **Listen and answer the questions about food.**

4

> **Speaking tip**
>
> In Speaking Part 1, try to speak slowly and clearly. Also, remember to smile – this will help you to relax.

1 Tell me about something you ate yesterday.

2 What do you like to eat for breakfast?

3 What is your favourite food?

4 Do you ever go on picnics? What food do you take with you?

5 Who cooks the meals in your home?

Reading

Read the short texts. For each question, choose the correct answer A, B or C.

1

Cafeteria: Thursday

There will be no hot meals served in the cafeteria this lunchtime.

A   The cafeteria is closed on Thursday.

B   Students can buy sandwiches in the cafeteria on Thursday.

C   Students should bring their own lunch to school on Thursday.

2

Strange food!

Have you ever eaten something strange or different? Where were you and why did you eat it?

Write an article for the school magazine about the strangest food you have eaten. The winner gets £20 and their article will appear in next month's magazine.

A   The magazine wants articles about students' favourite food.

B   Students who have not eaten an unusual food should not write an article.

C   Students who want to eat an unusual food should reply to the advertisement.

3

Hi Jude
I'm at the supermarket. I'm cooking pasta for dinner tonight. Are there any tomatoes and onions in the kitchen?
Thanks
Mum x

A   Mum wants Jude to check what food she needs to buy for dinner.

B   Mum wants Jude to cook pasta for dinner.

C   There are tomatoes and onions at home.

Reading tip

In Reading Part 1, you will read six different short texts. Think about what sort of text each one is. Is it an email, a text message, an advertisement or a notice? For an advertisement you will probably need to look for specific information. For an email or a text message you should think about how you would reply to it.

Grammar: Present perfect: *ever*

We use *ever* with the present perfect in questions and negatives to ask and answer about experiences.

Have you *ever eaten* something strange or different?

Write one or two sentences using present perfect to answer this question.

Listening

PART 2

For each question, write the correct answer in the gap. Write *one word*, or a *number*, or a *date* or a *time* in each gap.

You will hear a waitress talking to a customer about the menu.

MENU

Soup of the day:
(1) _____   £3.50

Sandwiches:
Cheese and (2) _____
Egg salad £ (3) _____

(4) _____ and chips £ (5) _____
Fish (6) _____ and rice £ 6.50

Opening times: 8 a.m. – (7) _____ p.m.

Listening tip

In Listening Part 2, you need to write a word, a number, a date or a time in each gap.

Times

Remember that *a.m.* means morning and *p.m.* means afternoon or evening.

Writing

PART 6

Write a note.

You have decided to make a special dinner tonight for your parents. You've found a meal that you want to make. You want your sister, Lucy, to help you. Write a note for your sister.

Say:

- that you want to cook tonight
- what you've decided to cook
- what food you will need to buy to make the meal and ask her to go to the supermarket with you.

Write **25 words** or more.

Unit 3 colours and time

Vocabulary

1 Unscramble the words and match.

1 clabk _____   a

2 eerng _____   b

3 rangoe _____   c

4 wobrn _____   d

5 pupler _____   e

6 eywlol _____   f

7 inpk _____   g

8 erd _____   h

9 rivels _____   i

10 ulbe _____   j

2 Complete the words in each sentence.

1 I get up at 7.00 in the m_____.

2 School finishes at 4.00 in the a_____.

3 In the UK, it gets cold in the w_____.

4 There are twelve m_____ in a year.

5 The stars are out at 12 m_____.

6 I eat my lunch at 12 n_____.

7 Summer comes after s_____.

8 There are seven d_____ in the week.

9 T_____ is the day after today.

10 Y_____ is the day before today.

3 Look at the photos and choose the best words to complete the texts.

1 In this photo, the sky is *golden / grey*.
I think it's the afternoon or evening.

2 In this photo, there is a boy skateboarding in the park. He's wearing jeans, a blue hat and a *light / dark* green jacket.

3 Look at the lovely big rabbit in this photo. It's a beautiful colour. It's *dark / pale* grey.

4 I really like this *dark / white / grey* sofa.

Speaking

Listen and answer the questions about colours and time.

6

1 What's your favourite colour?
2 Describe your hair and your eyes.
3 What different colours are there in your bedroom? Describe the furniture, floor, walls and curtains.
4 What did you do yesterday?
5 What do you like to do at the weekend?
6 What's your favourite month? Why is it your favourite?

Reading

1 Read the text about a new app.

For each question, choose the correct answer.

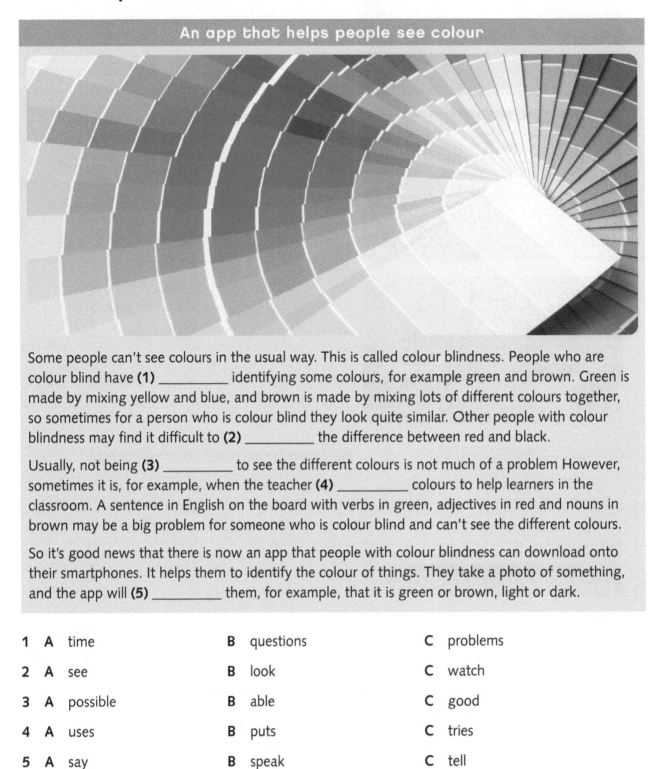

An app that helps people see colour

Some people can't see colours in the usual way. This is called colour blindness. People who are colour blind have **(1)** _____ identifying some colours, for example green and brown. Green is made by mixing yellow and blue, and brown is made by mixing lots of different colours together, so sometimes for a person who is colour blind they look quite similar. Other people with colour blindness may find it difficult to **(2)** _____ the difference between red and black.

Usually, not being **(3)** _____ to see the different colours is not much of a problem However, sometimes it is, for example, when the teacher **(4)** _____ colours to help learners in the classroom. A sentence in English on the board with verbs in green, adjectives in red and nouns in brown may be a big problem for someone who is colour blind and can't see the different colours.

So it's good news that there is now an app that people with colour blindness can download onto their smartphones. It helps them to identify the colour of things. They take a photo of something, and the app will **(5)** _____ them, for example, that it is green or brown, light or dark.

1	**A**	time	**B** questions	**C**	problems
2	**A**	see	**B** look	**C**	watch
3	**A**	possible	**B** able	**C**	good
4	**A**	uses	**B** puts	**C**	tries
5	**A**	say	**B** speak	**C**	tell

Grammar: Passive (present): when the object of a sentence is more important than the subject

Green *is made* by mixing yellow and blue.

Write a sentence using present passive to explain how to make the colour orange.

Listening

 For each question choose the correct answer A, B or C.

7   1   **You will hear a girl, Kate, talking about shopping.**

Why did Kate buy the jumper?

A   The colour was right.

B   It was dark.

C   It was pale.

2   **You will hear a boy giving directions to his house.**

What colour is the boy's house?

A   dark blue

B   pink

C   yellow

3   **You will hear two girls discussing earrings.**

Which do they like best?

A   the purple earrings

B   the blue earrings

C   the pink earrings

Writing

Write an email.

Your English pen friend, Poppy, has asked you to tell her about your daily routine. Write an email to Poppy.

Say:

- what time you get up and describe your morning routine
- what time you start and finish school
- what you do in the evenings.

Write **25 words** or more.

Writing tip

In Writing Part 6, you will be asked to write a message of 25 words or more, for example a note or email. There are three prompts. Make sure you write something for each prompt.

Vocabulary

1 Look at the family tree. Then complete the missing words in the sentences.

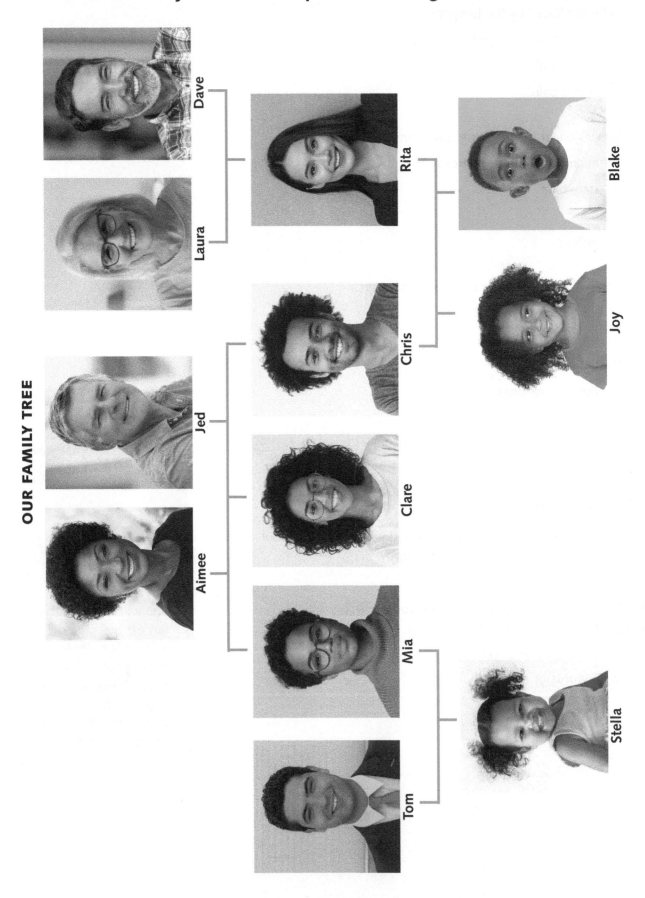

OUR FAMILY TREE

Dave

Laura

Rita

Blake

Joy

Jed

Chris

Clare

Aimee

Mia

Tom

Stella

1   Aimee is Jed's w_____.

2   Clare is Stella's a_____.

3   Chris is Mia's b_____.

4   Aimee and Jed are Mia, Clare and Chris's p_____.

5   Aimee and Jed are Stella's g_____.

6   Dave is Laura's h_____.

7   Joy and Blake are Chris and Rita's c_____.

8   Joy is Blake's s_____.

9   Stella is Joy and Blake's c_____.

10 Joy is Laura and Dave's g_____.

11 Blake is Laura and Dave's g_____.

12 Tom is Joy and Blake's u_____.

13 Rita is Laura and Dave's d_____.

14 Blake is Chris and Rita's s_____.

15 Stella, Joy and Blake are Aimee and Jed's g_____.

Grammar: **Possessives: to say who family members are**

Clare is Mia's sister.

Draw a simple family tree for your family. Then write a sentence using possessives to say who two or more people in your family are.

2 Look at the photo. Complete the description using the words from the box.

group	guests	husband	married	wife

The photo shows a **(1)** _____ of friends at a wedding party. Two of the people are

(2) _____. The **(3)** _____ is wearing a white dress and holding some flowers.

The **(4)** _____ is wearing a blue jacket and blue trousers. There are lots of **(5)** _____.

They all look very happy.

Speaking

Listen and answer the questions about family and friends.

8

1 Do you have any brothers or sisters?
2 Do you have any cousins?
3 Do you have a small or a large family?
4 Who is your best friend?
   What do you like to do together?
5 Do you have a pen friend?

Reading

Read the email from a girl to her new pen friend.

For each question, write the correct answer.

Write one word for each gap.

From: Amira
To: Mei

Hi Mei,

Thank you **(1)** _____ your email. I'm very excited to have a pen friend
in Hong Kong. I really like the photo of you and your grandparents. I haven't got
(2) _____ grandparents, but I'm attaching a photo of me with some of
(3) _____ family.

I'm the girl in the middle of the photo. I've got blonde hair and brown eyes. Next to me are
my two older sisters: Hana and Nadia. They're both teenagers. Have you **(4)** _____
any brothers or sisters? Are they older or younger **(5)** _____ you?

The two men in the photo are my dad and our neighbour, Mr Jeffries. My dad's the taller
man. Dad and Mr Jeffries **(6)** _____ best friends.

I've got to go now, but I'll write again soon and send more photos!

Amira

Listening

9 **You will hear Fred talking to his mother about a family picnic. What will each person bring or do?**

People	Bring or do
1 Auntie Jane	A bring Grandma
2 Mabel	B go shopping
3 Cousin John	C make sandwiches
4 Uncle Mike	D bring music
5 Mum	E bring games to play
	F make salads
	G bring chairs

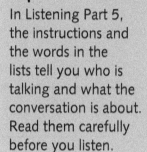

Listening tip

In Listening Part 5, the instructions and the words in the lists tell you who is talking and what the conversation is about. Read them carefully before you listen.

Writing

Write a story.

Look at the picture.

Write the story shown in the picture.

Write **12 words** or more.

Writing tip

In Writing Part 7, you need to look at the pictures and write a story. Try to write about:
• who is in the picture
• where they are
• and what they are doing.

Vocabulary

1 Complete the crossword

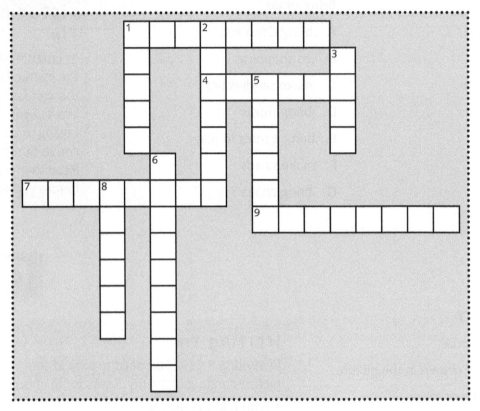

Across

1

4

7

9

Down

1

2

3

5

6

8

2 Read the invitation and choose the correct word to complete each gap.

Please come to my birthday party on Saturday 21 August!
There will be a (1) *musician / dancer* playing the guitar.
We will have a dancing (2) *competition / quiz*.
My mum and dad will cook a (3) *picnic / barbecue* in the garden and we can (4) *tent / camp* in the garden.
Bring your camera to take (5) *photos / video games*.
Kim

3 Use a verb from the box to complete each phrase. You will need to use some verbs more than once.

go   go to   have   join   listen to   play   ride   take

1 _____ a bicycle
2 _____ the beach
3 _____ a video game
4 _____ cycling
5 _____ on holiday
6 _____ or _____ music

7 _____ or _____ a picnic
8 _____ a barbecue
9 _____ the museum
10 _____ camping
11 _____ or _____ a club
12 _____ a photograph

Speaking

10
Listen and answer the questions about hobbies and leisure.

1 Do you have any hobbies?
2 What hobbies did you have when you were six?
3 What hobby would you like to try?
4 Do you go to any clubs? What clubs do you go to? Who do you go with?
5 Have you ever been on holiday? Where did you go? What did you do?

Speaking tip

Look at the language in the question. Try to use the same language in your answer.

What hobby **would you like to try**?

I **would like to try** photography, but I haven't got a camera.

Read the short texts. For each question, choose the correct answer A, B or C.

1

Photography club

Friday afternoon photography club will be on Wednesday at lunchtime in room A03 this week only.

A Photography club is usually on Fridays.

B Photography club is always on a Wednesday.

C There is a new photography club starting at school this week.

2

Radside Festival

Good for families

Bring your own tent

Food from around the world

Go to the festival if you want to

A learn to cook different food.

B sleep in a hotel.

C enjoy time with your children.

3

School quiz night

? ?

Ask your parents to buy tickets on the school website this weekend. We will give the tickets to you in your class on Monday.

A Students can buy tickets at school on Monday.

B The school quiz night is this weekend.

C Parents should buy tickets online.

Listening

PART 4

For each question, choose the correct answer A, B or C.

11

1   You will hear Jimmy talking to his grandma.

   What is Grandma's hobby?

   A   reading

   B   dancing

   C   cycling

2   You will hear a family trying to decide where to go.

   Where do they decide to go?

   A   the beach

   B   the shops

   C   the museum

3   You will hear two friends talking about their weekend.

   Where have they just been?

   A   at a campsite

   B   in a restaurant

   C   at a party

Grammar: Gerunds as subjects and objects

I like *cycling* in the park. (gerund as an object)

Cycling is good for you. (gerund as a subject)

Write two sentences using gerunds (*-ing*) to talk about a hobby. Write one sentence with the gerund as an object. Write another sentence with the gerund as the subject.

Writing

Write a text message.

You are meeting your English cousin, Oliver, on Saturday. Write a text message to Oliver to plan what you will do together.

• Ask Oliver what he would like to do this weekend.

• Make a suggestion about something you like doing on Saturdays.

• Tell Oliver what time you want to meet.

Write **25 words** or more.

Vocabulary

1 Listen and write the words in the correct places.

12

1 _____ 2 _____ 3 _____ 4 _____

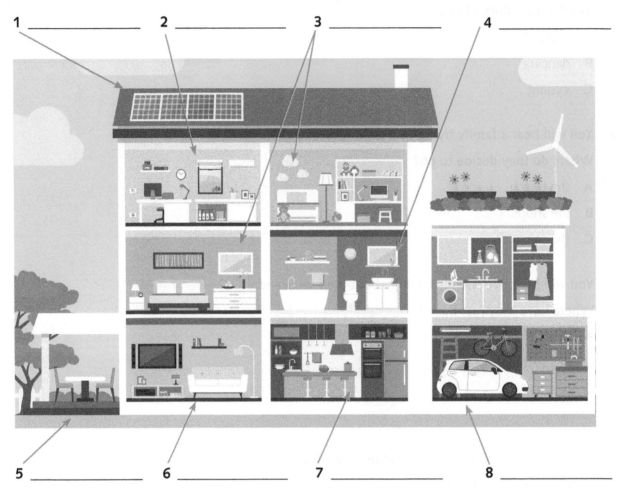

5 _____ 6 _____ 7 _____ 8 _____

2 Look at the home in Exercise 1. Are the sentences true or false?

1	This is an apartment.	True	False
2	There is a shelf in the living room.	True	False
3	There is some furniture in the garden.	True	False
4	The fridge is in the garage.	True	False
5	There is a shower in the bathroom.	True	False
6	There are two toilets in the home.	True	False
7	There is a computer in the office.	True	False
8	The office is downstairs.	True	False
9	There is a garden on the roof.	True	False
10	There is a bookcase in the office.	True	False

3 Choose the correct word from the box to complete each sentence.

> address   blanket   curtains   drawer   key   lights   rubbish   sink

1 After dinner, Lily put the dirty plates and bowls in the _____ .

2 Toby's _____ is 141A Radstock Villas, London.

3 Put the _____ in the bin.

4 I've just got new _____ for my bedroom window.

5 It was dark when we got home, so we turned on the _____ .

6 Issy put her clean clothes in her _____ .

7 I had to use my _____ to open the door because my parents were at work.

8 In the winter our flat is very cold, so I put a _____ on my bed at night.

Speaking

Listen and answer the questions about house and home.

13

1 Do you live in an apartment or a house?

2 How many rooms are there in your home?

3 What's your favourite room in your home and why?

4 Have you got a garden?

5 Describe your perfect home.

Speaking tip

If a question asks you to **imagine** or **describe** something that is not real, remember to use 'would + verb' in your reply.

Describe your perfect home.

My perfect home would have a swimming pool and a cinema.

Reading

Read the email from a girl to her friend.

For each question, write the correct answer.

Write one word for each gap.

From: Tina

To: Patrick

Hi Patrick,

I took this photo in my bedroom. Do you like it? These are my three favourite things.
This is my guitar. It was a present **(1)** _____ my grandma when I was seven.
I'm quite good at playing the guitar now. Can you **(2)** _____ an instrument?

This is my cat, Monty. Isn't he lovely? He's six years old and he loves to play. He also likes to sleep on my bed.

And those feet **(3)** _____ my teddy's feet. **(4)** _____ name is Forbes.
I got him **(5)** _____ I was one.

(6) _____ are your three favourite things? Can you take a photo and send it to me?

I've got to go now, but I'll write again soon!

Tina

Grammar: Demonstratives: to talk about people or things we can see

This is my cat, Monty. (Use *this* and *that* to talk about singular people or things)

These are my three favourite things. (Use *these* and *those* to talk about plural people or things)

Write a sentence describing what you can see in the room you are in.
Use *this/that/these/those*.

Listening

 For each question, choose the correct picture A, B or C.

14

1 What does Paul need to buy for his bedroom?

A
B
C

2 What *wouldn't* Emma have in her perfect house?

A
B
C

Writing

Write an email.

You want to invite your English friend, Luke, to see your new home. Write an email to Luke.

Say:

- that you would like to invite him to your home
- what day and time you would like him to come
- what your address is.

Write **25 words** or more.

Writing tip
For Writing Part 6, remember to start your message with *Dear*, *Hello* or *Hi*.
Dear Luke   Hello Holly   Hi Nora
Remember *Hi* is for informal writing.

Vocabulary

1 Complete the words.

1

b _ _ k

2

_ _ f _

3

c a _ _ l _

4
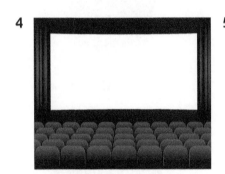
_ i n _ _ a

5

f a _ _ o _ y

6
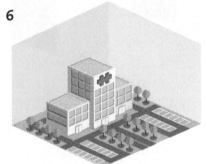
h o _ _ _ t a l

7

h _ t _ _

8

l i b _ _ _ y

9

_ _ s e _ _

10

p h _ _ _ _ _ _ _

11
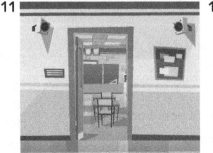
s _ _ o o _

12

t _ e a _ r e

2 Match each person (1–10) with the place (A–J) they want to go.

1	I want to watch a football match.	A	post office
2	I want to go swimming.	B	stadium
3	There is a problem with my car.	C	supermarket
4	I want to go dancing.	D	swimming pool
5	A person took my bag.	E	railway station
6	I want to send my uncle a birthday card by post.	F	garage
7	I'm going to visit my grandparents by train.	G	disco
8	I want to play tennis or badminton.	H	bookshop
9	I'm making dinner, but I haven't got any rice.	I	sports centre
10	I've just finished my book. I want to buy a new one.	J	police station

Speaking

PART 1

Listen and answer the questions about buildings.

15

1 Are the buildings where you live modern or old?

2 What's the biggest building where you live?

3 Do you prefer to go to a museum or a sports centre? Why?

4 Have you ever been to the theatre?

5 How often do you go to the cinema? Who do you go with?

Reading

Read the text about Balmoral Castle. For each question, choose the correct answer A, B or C.

The Queen's favourite place

Balmoral is a beautiful castle in Scotland. The original castle was built about 500 years ago. It was made from local Scottish stone, called granite. It was much smaller than it is now.

The castle is owned by the British royal family. In 1852, it was bought by the British queen, Victoria, and her husband, Albert. They added more buildings to the original castle to make it much bigger. Their granddaughter, Queen Mary, made the gardens bigger and more beautiful. She planted lots of flowers. She also made the castle more modern, and electricity was added to the building.

Today, the royal family still love Balmoral Castle and they go there every year for their summer holiday. The Queen says that it is her favourite place in the world!

Balmoral Castle is also very popular with tourists, who like to visit it when they are in Scotland. They hope to see the royal family there.

1 **How has Balmoral Castle changed since 1852?**

   A It is less popular.

   B It is bigger and more modern.

   C It is smaller and more modern.

2 **How did Queen Mary change Balmoral Castle?**

   A She invited lots of tourists to visit.

   B She added to the gardens.

   C She added more buildings.

3 **How does the Queen feel about Balmoral Castle?**

   A She likes it very much.

   B She doesn't like all the tourists.

   C She wants to make it bigger and more modern.

Reading tip

For Reading Part 3, read the title and quickly read the text first to find out what the topic is.

Grammar: **Passive (past simple): use it to talk about what happened to a building**

was/were + past participle

The original castle *was built* about 500 years ago. It *was made* from local Scottish stone, called granite.

Choose the correct words to complete the sentence.

*When **was / is** your house or apartment **build / built**?*

Now, answer the question. Write a complete sentence.

Listening

For each question, choose the correct answer A, B or C.

16 **You will hear Ava talking to her friend, Sam, about a day out.**

1 **Ava went to**

    A the museum.

    B the library.

    C the shopping centre.

2 **It is next to**

    A the hotel.

    B the shopping centre.

    C the café.

3 **Ava thought it was**

    A cool.

    B boring.

    C quiet.

Writing

Write an email.

Your Aunt Pauline and Uncle David from Australia are coming to visit you next month.
Write an email to your aunt and uncle.

In your email:

• say you are excited they are coming to visit

• tell them a building they should visit in your town, city or country

• explain why they should visit this building.

Write **25 words** or more.

Vocabulary

1 Fill in the words.

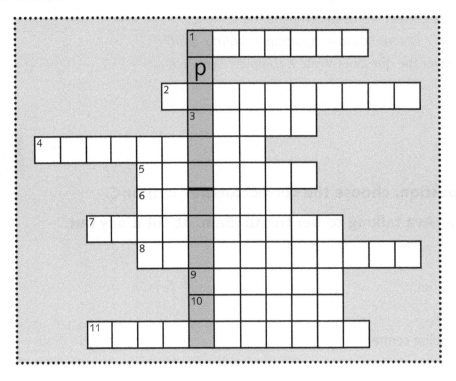

Clues

Find the missing words in blue. Complete the sentence.

You do sport at a _____ _____.

2 Write the words in the box in the correct place in the table below.

badminton baseball cycling fishing football hockey skiing swimming table tennis volleyball walking windsurfing

go...	play...

3 Look at the photo. Choose the best words to complete the text.

Hi, my name's Jay. I'm a **(1)** *member / game* of a cricket **(2)** *player / club*. We **(3)** *practise / enter* on Thursday evenings at the sports centre. In the photo you can see our **(4)** *coach / club*, Mr Ansari. He's very good at cricket and he teaches me a lot. You don't need much to play cricket. You only need a **(5)** *bat / racket* and a ball. You have to wear **(6)** *a bathing suit / kit* – ours is white – and trainers. In a game of cricket, a player from one **(7)** *team / family* **(8)** *throws / skates* the ball. Another player **(9)** *swims / hits* it. The other players try to **(10)** *run / catch* the ball. You have to be good at throwing, catching, hitting and running to play cricket.

Grammar: **Modals (1)** *can* **and** *have to*

Use *can* for ability
In this photo you *can* see Mr Ansari.

Use *have to* for obligation
You *have to* be good at throwing.

The modal comes before the main verb in a sentence.

Match sentences 1 and 2 with meaning A and B.
1   The school football team can win this game.
2   The school football team have to win this game.

A   The school football team won't continue in the competition if they lose this game.
B   The school football team are better than the other football team.

Speaking

PART 1

 **Listen and answer the questions about sport.**

17

1   What sports do you like? Is there a sport you don't like?
2   Is there a sport you play every week?
3   Are you a member of any sports clubs or teams?
4   Have you ever entered a sports competition?
5   Is there a sport you would like to try?

Reading

Read the three texts about the weekend. For each question, choose the correct answer A, B or C.

		Orla	Julia	Fran
1	Who watched a sports competition on the TV?	A	B	C
2	Who doesn't do the sport she watched?	A	B	C
3	Who can't do her sport well because of a hurt arm?	A	B	C
4	Whose team won their game?	A	B	C
5	Who had to travel to a different city to watch the game?	A	B	C
6	Who watched a family member in a competition?	A	B	C

Reading tip

In Reading Part 2, underline the key words in the questions *before* you read the texts. Then you will know what information you need to find in the texts.

For example *Who underline{watched} a underline{sports competition} on underline{TV}?*

What I did this weekend

Orla

This weekend, my dad and I travelled a long way to London to watch a rugby competition. We went by train from York. I like watching rugby. I don't play it, but my dad did when he was a teenager. You don't have to play a sport to like watching it! The game was exciting to watch. The players were really good and our team, the Frothies, won.

Julia

On Saturday, my family and I watched the football game Chelsea versus Liverpool on TV. I wanted Chelsea to win, but Liverpool won. They got four goals. I play football and I enjoy watching football, too. I play in a team on Tuesday and Thursday evenings. We're called the DST Cubs. I play football in the park with my friends after school, too. I love football.

Fran

On Sunday, I went to the swimming pool in our town with my grandma and my mum. We watched my sister in a swimming competition there. She's a really good swimmer. She has won four swimming prizes. Last year she was on television! I like swimming, too. I've entered one swimming competition, but I haven't won any prizes yet. I hurt my arm in January, so I can't swim very fast at the moment.

For each question, write the correct answer in the gap. Write *one word*, or *a number*, or *a date*, or *a time*.

You will hear a volleyball coach talking to her team.

Volleyball competition

Day: **(1)** ....

Place: Whitehawk **(2)** ....

Travel by: **(3)** ....

Leave school at: **(4)** ....

Bring: water and a **(5)** ....

Listening tip

In Listening Part 2, you need to write a word, number, date or time.

Times
Remember to write the times you hear in numerals.

half past five – 5.30

Writing

PART 6

Write an email.

There is a new sports club at school. You want to go and you would like your English friend, Matt, to come with you.

Write a text message to Matt.

• say you would like him to come to the new sports club at school

• explain what the new sports club is

• tell him when and where the new sports club is.

Write **25 words** or more.

writing tip

In Writing Part 6, think about who you are writing to. For example, you might begin an email to a teacher with *Dear...* and an email to a friend with *Hi...*

Vocabulary

1 Unscramble the words (1–9) and match with pictures (a–i).

1 kobo _____

a

2 snewaperp _____

b

3 mocic _____

c

4 umen _____

d

5 radyi _____

e

6 adrc _____

f

7 laime _____

g

8 tretel _____

h

9 zaagmine _____

i

2 Choose the correct word from the box to complete each sentence.

> advertisement bill form licence message notebooks
> passports postcard project text textbooks ticket

1 You can get a _____ to drive a motorbike at 16.

2 At the end of a meal, you ask the waiter for the _____.

3 My best friend went to New York last summer. She sent me a _____ with a picture of the Statue of Liberty on it.

4 My schoolbag is very heavy today because I have my maths, science and English _____ in it.

5 You can buy a _____ for the train online or at the railway station.

6 We write stories in English in our _____.

7 Mum had to fill in a _____ for me with my name, age and address, so that I could join the table tennis club.

8 In school, we are doing a _____ about buildings in our town.

9 I use my phone to _____ my friends.

10 Yesterday I sang the song from a new TV _____ for shampoo all day!

11 We showed our _____ before we got on the plane.

12 Your phone is making a noise. I think you have a text _____.

3 Look at the photo of the desk and read the words. Which things aren't on the desk?

1 tickets ☐

2 notes ☐

3 books ☐

4 a comic ☐

5 a passport ☐

6 a notebook ☐

7 a newspaper ☐

8 a form ☐

Speaking

PART 1

Listen and answer the questions about documents and texts.

1 Do you read comics? Did you read comics when you were younger?

2 What book are you reading? Are you enjoying it?

3 When do you send cards? Who do you send them to?

4 Can you tell me about a project you did at school?

5 How often do your parents read newspapers?

Reading

Read the text about Stan Lee.

For each question, choose the correct answer.

Stan Lee

Stan Lee was born New York, USA, in 1922. As a young child he loved reading books and **(1)** _____ movies. As a teenager he wrote stories and wanted to become a writer. In the 1950s, he began writing comic book stories for Marvel comics. He worked with the artist Jack Kirby and their first superheroes were the Fantastic Four. Jack Kirby **(2)** _____ the pictures and Stan Lee wrote the stories. The Fantastic Four was very **(3)** _____ so they wrote more stories about superheroes: the Hulk, Thor, Iron Man, X-Men, Spider-Man and Doctor Strange. They **(4)** _____ to put their superheroes together in the same stories, so they wrote the Avengers stories.

In 1972, Stan Lee stopped writing comic book stories but he continued to work with Marvel for the cinema, and he was in every Marvel **(5)** _____ – but you will only see him for one or two seconds!

Reading tip

In Reading Part 4, read the text quickly to get the main information and general meaning. Then read the text again more slowly. Look at all the possible answers for each question. Decide which is correct and think about why the other two answers are not correct. Think about the meaning of the words and the whole sentence.

1	A	looking	B	watching	C	checking
2	A	drew	B	wrote	C	made
3	A	wrong	B	happy	C	popular
4	A	wanted	B	liked	C	loved
5	A	film	B	comic	C	video

Listening

 For each question choose the correct answer A, B or C.

20 1 You will hear a girl, Patty, talking to her teacher about learning French.

   What does her teacher say she should do?

   A   listen to French music

   B   get a French pen friend

   C   watch French films

2 You will hear a boy and his mum.

   What has the boy forgotten to bring?

   A   his passport

   B   his notebook

   C   his phone

3 You will hear a teacher telling the class about a school trip.

   What is he asking parents to do?

   A   complete an online form

   B   send him an email

   C   send him a text message

Grammar: Modals (2) *must* and *should*

We use *should* to give advice.

You *should* listen to things in French.

We use *must* to talk about obligation.

You *must* ask your parents.

Remember: don't use *to*: you *must* ~~to~~ ask your parents, you *should* ~~to~~ listen

Write some advice for someone who is new at your school.

Writing

Write an email.

You are taking your English friend, Lulu, to your grandparents' house tomorrow.
Write an email to Lulu.

Say:

• where you want to meet

• what time you want to meet

• how you will travel and how much the tickets will cost.

Write **25 words** or more.

Vocabulary

1 Complete the crossword.

Across

3

4

7

8

9

Down

1

2

4

5

6

42

2 Match a verb from A to a phrase in B.

A

1 download
2 chat
3 click
4 write
5 answer
6 type
7 surf
8 take
9 look at
10 put

B

a on the mouse
b on a keyboard
c music from the internet
d the screen
e paper in the printer
f an email
g my mobile phone
h online with friends
i the internet
j a photograph

3 Choose the correct word from the box to complete each sentence.

call   email   envelope   information   password
photography   video game   website

1 I wrote a letter to my grandma and put it in an _____.

2 Jay is playing a _____ online with Kai.

3 The teacher is going to _____ us the answers to the homework tomorrow.

4 I love _____. Taking photographs is so much fun!

5 Never tell anyone your _____!

6 My mum found lots of _____ online about my new school.

7 My teacher has just put a video of our class trip on the school _____.

8 Lucy has to _____ her dad at 6.00.

Speaking

Listen and answer the questions about communication and technology.

21

1 What types of technology do you use every day?

2 Do you chat online with friends? What do you chat about?

3 Do you like taking photographs? What do you use to take them?

4 What websites do you like best?

5 What do you like doing on the internet?

Speaking tip

Try not to answer in one-word sentences. Use *and*, *but*, *so* and *because* to make longer sentences.

What types of technology do you use every day?

I use a computer every day to do my homework and I use my phone to chat online with my friends.

43

Reading

Read the three texts about an insect project. For each question, choose the correct answer A, B or C.

		Amy	Henry	Tom
1	Whose project was about a butterfly?	A	B	C
2	Who had help from their family?	A	B	C
3	Who didn't take any photos?	A	B	C
4	Who used a tablet in their project?	A	B	C
5	Who put their photos on the school website?	A	B	C
6	Who made a document on the computer?	A	B	C

Insect project

Amy

At school we're learning about insects, so our teacher asked us to do a project about an insect. We worked in groups of four. My group chose bees. We visited my uncle who has bees in his garden and is learning how to make honey. We took lots of photos on my phone. My mum helped me to email the photos to our teacher and she printed the photos out at school. Then we made a poster. We added lots of information about bees. We put the poster on the wall in our classroom for everyone to read.

Henry

Our teacher told us to work with a partner, so I did my project with my friend Kim. Kim likes butterflies, so we did our project on the biggest butterfly in the world: the Queen Alexandra's birdwing butterfly. We went online and found a few really good websites about it. We made lots of notes. Then we found some photos online, too. We decided to type all the information onto a document on the computer and add some of the photos. We printed it out and gave it to our classmates to read. I'd love to see one of these butterflies one day.

Tom

For our insect project we went into the school playground and looked for different insects. We found lots on the walls and in the grass. We counted how many we saw and we took photos using a school tablet. We used a ruler to find out which were the biggest and the smallest insects. In the classroom, we uploaded our photos to the class web page on the school website.

Grammar: Gerunds and infinitives

We *decided to* type all the information. (infinitive)

We *took* photos *using* the school tablet. (gerund)

Choose the correct options to complete the sentence.

I decided *draw / drawing / to draw* a picture *use / using / to use* a drawing app on my tablet.

Listening

22

For each question, write the correct answer in the gap.
Write *one word*, or *a number*, or *a date*, or *a time*.

You will hear a teacher talking to the class about computer club.

Computer club

Study in:	Computer Room A23
Day of the week:	**(1)** On ....
Club will be from:	**(2)** 2 April to .... June
Time:	**(3)** 4 p.m.– .... p.m.
Cost of club:	**(4)** £................. each week
Send an email to:	**(5)** Mrs ....

Listening tip

In Listening Part 2, you need to write a word, number, date or time.

Dates
Remember we use ordinal numbers to talk about dates.

1 May = *the first of May*

5 May = *the fifth of May*

21 May = *the twenty-first of May*.

Writing

Write an email.

You are going shopping with your mum and dad on Saturday and you would like to invite your English friend, Mark, to come with you.

Write an email to Mark.

Say:

• you want him to go shopping with you on Saturday

• what new item of technology you want to buy

• how you will travel there

Write **25 words** or more.

Vocabulary

1 Complete the words.

1

c l _ _ _ r _ _ m

2

_ _ _ k

3

r _ l _ _

4

s _ _ d _ _ t

5

t _ _ c h _ _

6

u _ _ v e _ _ i t y

2 Circle the correct words.

1

2

3

maths / biology   physics / geography   history / science

3 Match the words with their definitions.

> advanced beginner class classmate diploma exam
> homework lesson pupil subject term university

1 _____ : a place where you can study after you leave school

2 _____ : a test you take to show what you know about a subject

3 _____ : a group of students who learn together at school

4 _____ : school work that teachers give students to do at home in the evening
   or at the weekend

5 _____ : an area of knowledge that you study at school, for example, maths

6 _____ : a student who is in the same class as you at school

7 _____ : one of the children who goes to a school

8 _____ : a qualification a student may get at the end of their course of study

9 _____ : a time when you learn about a particular subject

10 _____ : one of the periods of time that a school year is divided into

11 _____ : someone who has just started to learn something

12 _____ : word to describe someone who is very good at something

Speaking

Listen and answer the questions about education.

23

1 What's your favourite subject at school?

2 Is there a subject you don't like?

3 How many English lessons do you have each week?

4 How many hours of homework do you have each week?

5 Where and when do you prefer to do your homework?

Speaking tip

In Speaking Part 1, remember that you can ask the examiner to repeat a question. Say *Could you say that again, please?*

Reading

Read the text about Morgan's school.

For each question, choose the correct answer A, B or C.

My classroom
By Morgan, age 8

I live in Australia. I live on a farm with my parents and my two brothers. Our farm is a long way from a school so we learn at home. I have a desk in my bedroom and I usually work there, but sometimes my classroom is my kitchen and sometimes it's my garden! I have online lessons with my teacher and my classmates every Monday and Friday, but we never meet in a real classroom. We study all the usual subjects – maths, English, science, history, geography and art. I love art. We have tests that my teacher emails to my parents once a term for each subject.

I also have a music teacher. I'm learning to play the violin. I have online music lessons once a week, and I practise on my own at home every day. We don't do sport online as a class, but my brothers and I always play football after school. And I'm learning to horse-ride.

1   **Where does Morgan have his classes?**

A   at school

B   at home

C   at university

2   **How often does Morgan see his classmates online?**

A   once a week

B   twice a week

C   three times a week

3   **What subject doesn't Morgan study online?**

A   sport

B   English

C   music

Reading tip

In Reading Part 3, read all the possible answers and decide why two aren't correct before you choose which one is correct.

Grammar: Adverbs of frequency: *always, usually, often, sometimes, never*

We use adverbs of frequency to talk about how often we do something.
Sometimes my kitchen is my classroom.

We can also say the *number of times* we do something every day, week, month or year.
I go to school *five times* a week.

Complete this sentence so that it is true for you.

I go to school _____ times a week and I _____ have homework at the weekend.

Listening

24

For each question, choose the correct answer A, B or C.

You will hear a teacher talking about a student.

1   The teacher is talking to

A   another student.

B   another teacher.

C   a parent.

2   Lottie

A   always does her homework.

B   usually does her homework.

C   never does her homework.

3   Last week's homework was for

A   science.

B   maths.

C   English.

> **Listening tip**
>
> In Listening Part 3, you will hear two people speaking. The answers could come from either speaker.

Writing

Write an email.

Your new English neighbour, Peter, is joining your class tomorrow. Write him an email.

Say:

• what lessons you have tomorrow

• who your teacher is

• how often you have homework.

Write **25 words** or more.

Vocabulary

1 Fill in the words.

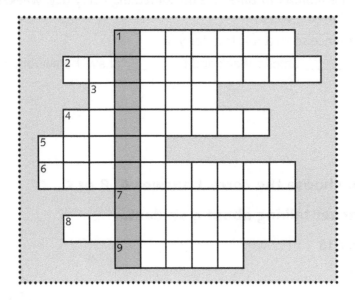

Clues

Find the missing word in blue. Complete the sentence.

There are lots of types of music, such as hip hop, pop and _____ .

2 Look at the photo. Tick the instruments you see.

drum	☐
piano	☐
keyboard	☐
guitar	☐
violin	☐

3 Complete the words.

1 A person who paints paintings is a p_____.

2 A person who sings songs is a s_____.

3 A person who acts in movies is an a_____.

4 A person who plays a musical instrument is a m_____.

5 A person who dances is a d_____.

6 A person who takes photographs is a p_____.

Speaking

25

Look at the photos that show different types of entertainment. Listen and answer the questions.

Speaking tip

In Speaking Part 2, you will see some pictures. Talk about **all** the pictures in your answers. Say which ones you like/ don't like and give your reasons. Use the word *because* for reasons.

1 Which of these types of entertainment do you like? Why?

2 Which of these types of entertainment don't you like? Why not?

3 Which is more fun, watching a show or being in a show? Why?

4 Do you prefer going out or staying at home for entertainment? Why?

Reading

Read the short texts. For each question, choose the correct answer A, B or C.

1

NOW ON FIRST FLOOR:

→ **Painting exhibition**

→ **Photography show**

→ **Video games to try!**

Go upstairs if you want to

A   paint a picture.

B   practise taking photographs.

C   play video games.

2

MUSIC LESSONS TODAY

Students who have forgotten to bring musical instruments with them today should go to normal lessons.

A   Students with musical instruments are not going to do normal lessons.

B   Students have to decide if they want to bring musical instruments to school today.

C   Students with musical instruments should go to normal lessons.

3

From: George

To: Sam

Hey!

I'm going to take the train at 7.55 p.m. to the rock concert tonight. Do you want to travel with me?

A   George can't travel with Sam to the concert.

B   George has bought a train tickets for Sam.

C   George wants to know if Sam wants to go on the train with him to the concert.

Grammar: **Future with *going to*: to talk about future plans.**

My plan: I'm *going to take* the train at 7.55 p.m. tonight.

Write a sentence about a plan you have for this week, using *going to*.

Listening

26

You will hear Lily talking to her dad about the weekend.

What is she doing with each of her friends?

People		Activity	
1	Jane	**A**	Go dancing
2	Zack	**B**	Play chess
3	Billy	**C**	Go to a dance show
4	Rebecca	**D**	Play a video game
5	Issy	**E**	Practise drums
		F	Play a board game
		G	Listen to music

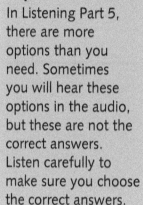

Listening tip

In Listening Part 5, there are more options than you need. Sometimes you will hear these options in the audio, but these are not the correct answers. Listen carefully to make sure you choose the correct answers.

Writing

Write an email.

Your parents have invited your English friend, Sid, to come to a concert with your family this weekend. Write an email to Sid.

Say:

• that he is invited to the concert
• what sort of music the concert is
• when and where the concert is.

Write **25 words** or more.

Writing tip

In Writing Part 6, if you are asked to give a date or time, remember we use *at* + time (at 5 p.m.), *on* + day (on Monday) and *in* + month (in July).

Vocabulary

1 Circle nine words in the wordsearch and write them under the correct photos.

t	y	r	h	a	p	p	y	q	o
b	u	r	u	n	h	a	p	y	
o	n	l	n	o	i	b	o	s	t
r	g	o	g	y	n	o	i	s	y
e	q	z	r	s	p	l	l	r	o
d	m	r	y	e	d	d	y	b	d
t	y	y	e	s	t	r	o	n	g
t	i	r	e	d	g	z	u	n	n
u	a	n	g	r	y	g	n	d	u
q	m	k	t	z	a	n	g	r	i

1
_____

2
_____

3
_____

4
_____

5
_____

6
_____

7
_____

8
_____

9
_____

2 Circle the correct word in each sentence.

1 The maths test was *difficult / tired*.

2 The rabbit was *married / soft*.

3 Mum said, 'Be *pretty / quiet* because the baby is asleep.'

4 I'm *interested / clever* in animals.

5 I don't know where my friends are. I'm *alone / old*.

6 I'm *wrong / sorry* that I broke the window.

7 My uncle is a *famous / useful* actor.

8 Ailsa has got to do her homework, cook dinner and tidy her bedroom. She's very *busy / terrible*.

9 Would you like to try some chocolate? It's *unhappy / free* – you don't have to pay any money.

10 There was a snake in Dina's bedroom – she was *afraid / strange*.

3 Match the sentence halves.

1 I'm going to bed now because

2 Mum's planted lots of flowers in the garden, so

3 Lara isn't at school today because

4 I'm worried about the English test today because

5 William is very clever so

6 Our neighbours have bought a second house;

a it's lovely.

b it's very important.

c I'm tired.

d I think they are rich.

e she isn't well.

f he always gets the best marks in the homework.

Speaking

Listen and answer the questions about personal feelings, opinions and experiences.

27

1 What makes you happy?

2 What are you afraid of?

3 What is the most interesting thing you have done?

4 Would you like to be famous? Why or why not?

5 Can you tell me about a time when you were lucky?

Reading

For each question, write the correct answer.

Write ONE word for each gap.

From: Jed

To: Steven

Hi Steven,

How is your holiday? I'm at my uncle's house. I want to tell you about what happened yesterday.

I was walking in the mountains **(1)** _____ my uncle. The weather was beautiful. The sky was clear, with no clouds. It was very hot. I was wearing shorts and a T-shirt. The birds were singing and the sun was shining.

But then **(2)** _____ weather suddenly changed! It was strange! Suddenly, it was raining and the sky was black. My uncle was worried **(3)** _____ we ran to a house. The people in the house were very kind. They let us wait in the house for more **(4)** _____ an hour. And they gave us some food **(5)** _____ we were very hungry.

Then the rain stopped and the skies were blue again!

Tell me about your summer.

Jed

Reading tip

In Reading Part 5, remember you only need to write ONE word in each gap and that your spelling must be correct. Check your answers carefully!

Grammar: Past continuous: to talk about an action in the past that continued

Often a short action 'stops' this longer action.
I *was walking* in the mountains.
The birds were *singing* and the sun was *shining*.

Choose the correct forms of the verbs to complete the sentences.
It *rained/ was raining* and the birds *sang/ were singing*.
I *was walking /walked* home when I *was seeing / saw* my friend John.

Listening

 For each question, choose the correct answer A, B or C.

You will hear a girl, Mona, talking to her friend Jay about a person she met.

1 The person Mona met was

   A a painter.

   B famous.

   C a dancer.

2 Mona thought the painting was

   A bad.

   B pleasant.

   C amazing.

3 The painting was of

   A old people.

   B Mona.

   C young people.

> **Listening tip**
>
> In Listening Part 3, think about how each speaker feels. What positive and negative words do they use?

Writing

Write an email.

You have a plan to go to your English friend Ava's house this evening but you are very tired. Write a text message to Ava.

Say:

- how you are feeling and explain why
- you don't want to meet this evening and apologise
- what day you can meet up instead.

Write **25 words** or more.

> **Writing tip**
>
> Use *Let's...* and *Shall...* to make suggestions.
>
> *Let's* go to the ice cream café on Thursday after school.
>
> *Shall* we go to the park?

Vocabulary

1 Unscramble the words and match.

1 leagilv _____

a

2 virre _____

b

3 aywailr _____

c

4 keal _____

d

5 maintonu _____

e

6 dislan_____

f

7 trofes _____

g

8 pacsmite _____

h

9 chabe _____

i

10 yks _____

j

2 Match the words with their definitions.

| area | field | forest | path | rainforest | wood |

1 _____: a very large area of trees

2 _____: a smaller area of trees

3 _____: a long narrow piece of ground for people to walk along

4 _____: a piece of land or space

5 _____: a thick forest of tall trees that grows in places that are hot and have a lot of rain

6 _____: a piece of land where farmers grow crops or keep animals

3 Look at the photo. Tick the things you can see.

1	a rainforest ☐	4	hills ☐	7	the sea ☐	10	a path ☐
2	roads ☐	5	a campsite ☐	8	a lake ☐	11	a village ☐
3	a forest ☐	6	a beach ☐	9	mountains ☐	12	a river ☐

🎧 Speaking   PART 2

29

Look at the photos that show different places in the countryside. Listen and answer the questions.

1 Which of these places do you like best? Why?

2 Which of these places don't you like? Why not?

3 What different activities can you do in each of these places? Which do you think are the most fun?

4 Where would you prefer to go on holiday? Why?

59

Reading

1 **Read the three texts about a school trip. For each question, choose the correct answer A, B or C.**

	Emma	Jack	Stan
1 Who went swimming in the sea?	A	B	C
2 Who went to a village?	A	B	C
3 Who had a barbecue for lunch?	A	B	C
4 Who went by train?	A	B	C
5 Who went onto an island?	A	B	C
6 Who didn't enjoy their school trip?	A	B	C

School Trip

Emma

My class went on a school trip to the countryside. We went by bus. It took two hours. We went to a big lake in the mountains. We had a windsurfing lesson on the lake in the morning, and then we went on a boat to the island in the centre of the lake. Our teachers cooked a barbecue on the island for lunch. We had chicken, fish and vegetables. It was delicious! Then, we all swam back across the lake to the bus. The water was quite cold, but it was a great school trip.

Jack

Our school trip was really boring! We went by train to the countryside. The train went through lots of fields so there wasn't anything to look at, except for cows! I played on my phone all the way there. We arrived in a small village called Trent. It was very old and boring. There was nothing to do. There was only one small shop. We wanted to buy some sweets but the teachers didn't let us. We walked around and looked at the buildings and we drew some of them. Then we went to someone's house and they cooked us lunch. It was pasta. I don't like pasta. Then we got back on the train and came home.

Stan

For our school trip we went to the countryside. We went by bus. It only took 45 minutes. We went to a big forest and we walked for about three hours. It was great. We stopped for about half an hour to have a picnic. After three hours, we arrived at a beautiful beach. At the beach we all went swimming and surfing. It was amazing. I fell asleep on the bus back to school because I was so tired after all the activities.

Listening

30

For each question, choose the correct picture A, B or C.

1 Where is Gill's cousin working now?

A

B

C

2 Where are they going to have a picnic?

A

B

C

Grammar: *Shall* for suggestions and offers

Use *shall + we* to make suggestions
Shall we go to the lake?

Use *shall + I* to make offers
Shall I make some sandwiches?

The modal comes before the main verb.

Write one suggestion and one offer:

1 It's hot. _____ open a window for you?

2 It's a lovely day. _____ go to the park?

Listening tip

In Listening Part 1, listen and choose the best answer. Then listen again and check your answer.

Writing

Write an email.

At the weekend you went to the countryside. Tell your friend Kate about it. Write her an email.

Say:

- who you went with
- where you went and what you did
- what it was like.

Write **25 words** or more.

Vocabulary

1 Complete the crossword. Then answer the question.

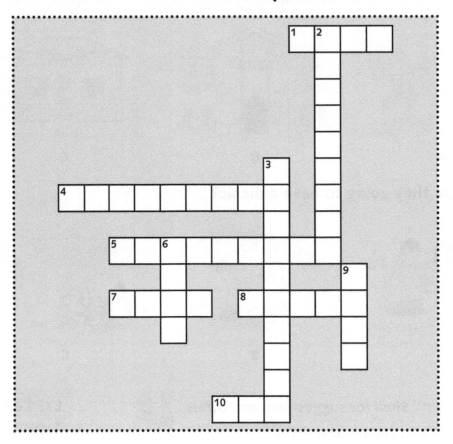

Across

1

4

5

7

8

10

Down

2

3

6

9

What's the difference between a ship and a boat?

_____

2 Choose the correct words from the box to complete the definitions.

1 A person who drives a bus, car or train is a _____.

2 A person who flies a plane is a _____.

3 A person who travels around a place to find out what it is like is an _____.

4 A person who repairs cars is a _____.

5 A person who helps people who are on holiday or shows them around a place is a _____.

6 A person who is travelling in a vehicle, such as a bus, train or plane, but is not driving it is a _____.

3 Circle the correct words.

1

traffic lights / machines

2

luggage / tyre

3

roundabout / bridge

4

platform / airport

5

mirror / motorway

6

suitcase / backpack

Speaking   PART 1

Listen and answer the questions about travel and transport.

31

1 How do you travel to school?

2 What transport do you not like using?

3 Have you ever travelled by train or plane? Where did you go?

4 Do many visitors come to your country?

5 Would you like to be an explorer? Why or why not?

Reading

Read the short texts. For each question, choose the correct answer A, B or C.

1

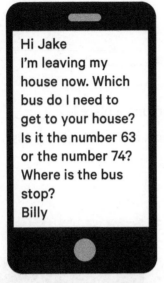

Hi Jake
I'm leaving my house now. Which bus do I need to get to your house? Is it the number 63 or the number 74? Where is the bus stop?
Billy

A Jake is at Billy's house.

B Billy is on the bus.

C Billy is going to Jake's house.

2

10.15 TRAIN TO GRETNA

PLEASE NOTE THIS TRAIN IS DELAYED AND WILL NOW LEAVE AT 10.35 FROM PLATFORM 5 AND NOT FROM PLATFORM 7. GO TO THE TICKET OFFICE IF YOU WANT MORE INFORMATION.

Passengers who want to take the 10.15 train to Gretna must

A wait for an hour.

B go to a different platform.

C go to the ticket office.

Grammar: Interrogatives (*Wh-* questions)

Where is the bus stop?
Which bus do I need to get?

Use different *Wh-* question words to ask for different information.
Where? = place
Who? = person
When? = time
Why? = reason
Whose? = person a thing belongs to
Which? = one from more than one possibility
What? = object or piece of information

Match the questions to the answers.

1 Who are you going to the cinema with?
2 Whose coat is this?
3 When does the film start?
4 Where shall we meet?
5 What number is your apartment?

a 5A.
b At half past seven.
c At the bus stop.
d It's mine.
e Rachel and Fiona.

For each question, choose the correct answer A, B or C.

32

1   You will hear a teacher talking about a school trip.

   What time will the class leave?

   A   1:30

   B   7:30

   C   8:00

2   You will hear a man and a woman on a car journey.

   Where do they decide to stop?

   A   at a supermarket

   B   at a petrol station

   C   in a town

3   You will hear a father talking to his children.

   How will they travel to the festival?

   A   by car

   B   by train

   C   by bus

> ### Listening tip
>
> In Listening Part 4, there is often a **change of plan**. Listen for words and phrases in bold: *There is a problem with ...*, so *now* we will ... and *not ...*'
>
> OR
>
> Man: Let's go to the City Café.
>
> Woman: OK. (This is the first plan.)
>
> Man: **Wait!** The Park Café is nearer.
>
> Woman: *Oh yes! Let's go there instead.* (change of plan)

Grammar: **Interrogatives (with** *be***)**

Use the verb *to be* to make yes/no questions. The verb comes at the beginning of the question.

Is there a petrol station near here?

Use short form answers: **Yes***, there is.* / **No***, there isn't.*

Write answers that are true for you.

1   Are you a boy?

2   Are you a girl?

3   Is it Wednesday today?

4   Is it Thursday today?

Writing

PART 6

Write an email.

You are going to visit your English friend, Milo. He lives in a different city. Write an email to Milo.

In your email,

• say what day you will go and how you will travel

• say when and where you will arrive

• ask him to meet you.

Write **25 words** or more.

Vocabulary

1 Complete the words.

1

f _ _ _ b _ _ _ pl _ _ _ _

2

t _ _ _ her

3

t _ _ _ is pl _ _ _ _

4

do _ _ _ _ _

5

_ oo_

6

w_ _t _ _

7

s _ _ g _ r

8

fa _ _ _ r

9

pol _ _ _ off _ _ _ _

10

d _ _ t _ _ t

11

cl _ _ _ e _

12

_ rt _ _ t

2 Choose the correct words to complete the texts.

This is a photo of my mum at work. She works in **(1)** *a café / an office*. She's a **(2)** *businesswoman / pilot*. She sits at a big **(3)** *desk / factory* and writes **(4)** *emails / diaries* on her computer. She also goes to lots of **(5)** *messages / meetings*. She doesn't wear **(6)** *an occupation / a uniform*. She doesn't often have a lunch break, but she really likes her job!

This is a photo of my big brother Dan at work. Dan's sixteen. He works in **(7)** *an office / a shop* on Saturdays. He's a **(8)** *shop assistant / shopper*. His **(9)** *instructions / uniform* is an orange T-shirt and black trousers. He has to help the **(10)** *guests / customers*. He **(11)** *is / works* from 9.00 a.m. to 5 p.m. Dan loves taking photos, so when he's older he wants to be a **(12)** *photographer / mechanic*.

Speaking

PART 1

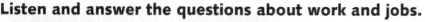

Listen and answer the questions about work and jobs.

33

> **Speaking tip**
>
> In Speaking Part 1, if you make a mistake, you can correct yourself. This is a good way of showing the examiner that you know the correct word or grammar. Be confident, say *'No, that's not right. I mean …'*

1 What jobs do some of the people in your family have?

2 What do you think is the best job? Why?

3 What do you think is the worst job? Why?

4 Is working in an office a good job?

5 Where is a good place to work? Why?

Reading

Read the text about Millie's grandma.

For each question, choose the correct answer A, B or C.

My grandma
By Millie, age 9

My grandma has had lots of different jobs since she was young. She finished school when she was 16 and she worked in a factory. She didn't like the factory. The work was very hard, and she didn't like her manager. So she left her job and got a job on a farm. She liked the countryside and she liked all the animals. She also liked the farmer and the other people she worked with. They all lived together in the farmhouse. She picked fruit and vegetables on the farm. It was good in the summer, but cold in the winter.

After the farm, she went back to the city and worked as a cleaner in a hospital. She liked talking to all the staff, especially the nurses. Sometimes she talked to the sick people and their families too. She liked the hospital so much that she decided to go to college and become a nurse. She got her diploma and got a job in another hospital. She worked there for 25 years and she became a manager. She was a very good nurse.

Grandma left her job five years ago, but she sometimes goes back to the hospital to visit the other nurses and the doctors. She's still got her nurse's uniform and sometimes she lets me put it on, and I pretend to be a nurse.

1 How did Millie's grandma feel about her job on the farm?

   A She didn't like the other workers.

   B She liked the other workers but didn't like her boss.

   C She liked everything but it was cold in the winter.

2 What was her grandma's first job at the hospital?

   A She was a cleaner.

   B She was a nurse.

   C She was a doctor.

3 Why did Millie's grandma go to college?

   A to become a manager

   B to become a nurse

   C to become a doctor

Reading tip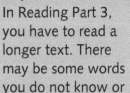

In Reading Part 3, you have to read a longer text. There may be some words you do not know or remember.

Read the whole sentence and think what the word might mean to make the sentence make sense.

Grammar: **Past simple: to talk about finished actions in the past**

She *finished* school when she was six.

Regular past simple verbs: + -ed
work – worked She *worked* in a factory.

Negative past simple: + *didn't* before the main verb
She *didn't* like the factory.

Write one positive and one negative sentence about the hobbies your parents did when they were younger. Use past simple.

Remember some verbs are irregular in the past tense:

present simple	past simple
I *am* a doctor.	I *was* a doctor.
I *go* to school.	I *went* to school.

Listening

PART 2

For each question, write the correct answer in the gap. Write *one word*, or *a number*, or *a date*, or *a time*.

You will hear a teacher telling her class about a job.

Job advert

Job: (1) ....

Number of children needed: (2) ....

Age of children needed: (3) 7– .... years old

Hair colour needed: (4) ....

Money: (5) £ ....

Writing

PART 7

Write a story.

Look at the picture.

Write the story shown in the picture.

Write **12 words** or more.

writing tip

When you write about the main event in a picture, use the present continuous tense. For example: *She is working at home.*

Vocabulary

1 Circle eight words in the wordsearch and write them under the correct photos.

l	o	b	t	r	h	s	w	m	a
a	i	r	p	o	r	t	n	a	a
s	s	i	k	a	i	a	m	r	a
q	u	d	e	d	t	t	e	k	e
u	g	g	l	k	h	i	e	e	p
a	o	e	r	p	o	o	v	t	b
r	p	r	i	f	e	n	k	g	o
e	c	a	r	p	a	r	k	j	x
p	l	a	y	g	r	o	u	n	d
c	c	d	f	r	a	c	x	p	y

1

_____

2

_____

3

_____

4

_____

5

_____

6

_____

7

_____

8

_____

2 Match each person (1–5) with the place (A–E) they want to go.

1 (I want to get a bus to the town square.)   **A**   the zoo

2 (I want to see some animals.)   **B**   the park

3 (I'm going by plane to Italy.)   **C**   the bus stop

4 (I need some petrol for my car.)   **D**   the petrol station

5 (I'm taking my dog for a walk.)   **E**   the airport

3 Match the words with their definitions.

| bus station   city centre   corner   motorway |
| roundabout   town   underground |

1 _____: the middle of a city

2 _____: a place with many streets, buildings and shops, where people live and work

3 _____: a place in a town or city where there are lot of buses that go to lots of different places

4 _____: the point where a road meets another road

5 _____: a circle in the road that drivers must drive round

6 _____: a railway system in a city which travels below the ground

7 _____: a wide road that allows cars to travel very fast over a long distance

Speaking

Listen and answer the questions about towns and cities.

35

1 Do you live in a town or city?

2 What is your favourite place to go in a city? Why?

3 Is there a bus station where you live? Is there a railway station or an airport?

4 How often do you go to a park or a playground?

5 Tell me something about the street where you live.

Speaking tip

Remember, in Speaking Part 1 don't answer with one word.

For example:

Do you live in a town or city?

No. ✗

No, I don't live in a town or a city. I live in a village. ✓

Reading

Read the text about Venice.

For each question, choose the correct answer.

Venice

Venice is a beautiful city in Italy. What makes Venice so special is that it doesn't have roads in the old **(1)** _____ of the city. Instead it has rivers, so people **(2)** _____ around the city by boat. There are about 160 rivers. The widest and most important river in Venice is called the Canal Grande. It is between the old and the new areas of the city and it has four bridges. The oldest bridge is the famous Rialto Bridge. The other bridges are the Ponte dell'Academia and the Ponte degli Scalzi. They are **(3)** _____ very old. The fourth bridge is more **(4)** _____. It is called Ponte delle Costituzione and it goes from the railway station to the bus station. There are 435 bridges in Venice. People like walking around the small streets in old Venice. There are lots of squares to sit in. The **(5)** _____ famous square is called St Mark's Square.

1	**A**	town	**B**	part	**C**	place
2	**A**	travel	**B**	walk	**C**	fly
3	**A**	even	**B**	and	**C**	also
4	**A**	modern	**B**	new	**C**	big
5	**A**	most	**B**	more	**C**	other

Reading tip

In Reading Part 4, after you have completed the gaps, read the text again. Does it make sense?

Grammar: Numbers: cardinal and ordinal

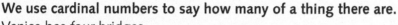

We use cardinal numbers to say how many of a thing there are.
Venice has *four* bridges.

With numbers that are more than 100 we say:
One hundred and...
There are about *160* rivers. (one hundred and sixty)

We use ordinal numbers to say the position of a thing in a list.
The *fourth* bridge is the Ponte delle Costituzione. (There are at least four bridges.)

Choose the correct forms of the numbers to complete the sentences.
There are *two / second* railway stations in my city. The *one / first* is next to the stadium.

Listening

PART 5

36

You will hear a boy, Lewis, talking to his mum about his school trip. Where did the people in his class want to go?

People		Activity	
1	Isaac	A	railway station
2	Lewis	B	bridge
3	Dina	C	underground
4	Jay	D	zoo
5	Mr Philips	E	park
		F	market
		G	playground

Writing

PART 6

Write an email.

You are going to the city centre with your mum and dad tomorrow. You would like to invite your English friend, Sara, to come with you. Write an email to Sara.

Say:

- you are going to the city and you would like her to come with you
- how you will travel to the city and where you will arrive in the city
- where you will go in the city.

Write **25 words** or more.

> **writing tip**
>
> When you write about places, try to add more detail about where a place is. For example:
>
> *The bus station is next to the market.*
>
> *The zoo is near the park.*

Vocabulary

1 Complete the crossword.

Across

3

5

7

8

Down

1

2

4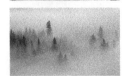

6

7

2 Unscramble the months. Remember to start each month with a capital letter.

1 ruanjay _____

2 beufarry _____

3 rialp _____

4 enuj _____

5 stugau _____

6 temserbep _____

7 cootreb _____

8 beedmerc _____

3 Write the missing months from Exercise 2.

1 _____

2 _____

3 _____

4 _____

4 Look at the photo. Complete the description with the words from the box. There are THREE words that you don't need.

> cold   hot   ice   snow   snowboarding
> weather   white   windsurfing   windy

It's December. This is a photo of my road this morning. It's a very **(1)** _____ day here today.
I'm wearing my red ski jacket and my hat and gloves. There's a lot of **(2)** _____ on the trees and on the road. The sky is grey and the forest is **(3)** _____. We have to walk to school because there is **(4)** _____ on the roads and it's dangerous for cars. I like this **(5)** _____ because after school I will go **(6)** _____ with my friends!

Grammar: Adjectives

We can use adjectives to describe a noun using the verb *be*.
Noun + *am/is/are* + adjective
The sky is *grey*.

When using adjectives, often the adjective comes before the noun.
I'm wearing my *red* ski jacket.

Write two sentences about the boots using adjectives. One sentence should use the verb *be* and one sentence should have the adjective before the noun.

Speaking

PART 1

Listen and answer the questions about weather and months.

37

1   What is the weather like today?

2   What is your favourite weather? Why? What do you like to do in this weather?

3   What month is your birthday?

4   Which is your favourite month? Why?

5   How often does it snow where you live?

Reading

Read the email from Laura to her friend Stella.

For each question, write the correct answer.

Write one word for each gap.

From: Laura

To: Stella

Hi Stella,

How are you? I hope you are having a lovely time with **(1)** _____ cousins in Australia. What's the weather like in Brisbane today? **(2)** _____ it hot and sunny? Are you going to the beach?

It's a horrible, wet day here today. The sky is dark and grey. There was a big thunderstorm last night. It started at midnight and didn't stop **(3)** _____ three o'clock in the morning. It was very loud. I couldn't sleep. I hate February **(4)** _____ England. I want to be in Australia with you!

I've got to go now. Send **(5)** _____ a photo of your trip.

Laura

Grammar: Adjectives (order)

Often we use two adjectives to describe a noun.
It's a *horrible, wet* day.

Use adjectives in this order:

opinion	size	quality	shape	age	colour	noun
horrible,		*wet*				*day*
lovely,	*big*					*clouds*

Write a sentence about the weather today. Use an opinion adjective and one other adjective.

76

Listening

 For each question, choose the correct picture A, B or C.

38   1   When is the man getting married?

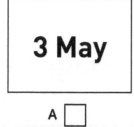

3 May	13 June	30 July

A ☐   B ☐   C ☐

2   Why can't the man and woman go out?

A ☐   B ☐   C ☐

Listening tip

We can add a *y* to some nouns to make adjectives. Watch out for the spelling!

sun → sunny   cloud → cloudy   wind → windy   fog → foggy

Writing

Write an email.

You are going for a walk with your English friend, James, on Saturday. Write an email to James.

Say:

- where you are going to walk
- what the weather will be
- what clothes or accessories James should bring.

Write **25 words** or more.

Writing tip

At the end of your email or message use a phrase such as:

See you soon.

See you on (Saturday).

Bye for now.

Vocabulary

1 Listen and write the words in the correct places.

39

1 _____   2 _____   3 _____

4 _____   5 _____   6 _____

2 Complete the words.

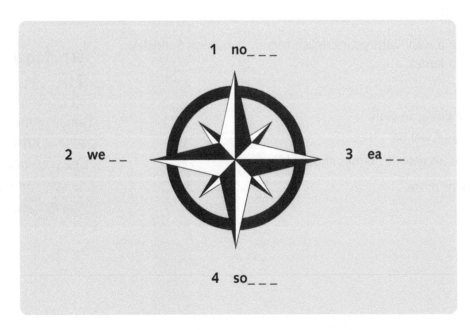

1 no_ _ _

2 we _ _

3 ea _ _

4 so_ _ _

3 Choose words from the box to complete each sentence.

> autumn   bees   desert   fire   grow   hill   ice
> moon   rabbit   stars   wool

1 Trees _____ in the forest.

2 At night, you often see the _____ and the _____ in the sky.

3 My jumper is made of _____.

4 I rode a camel in the _____ in North Africa.

5 My parents made a _____ on the beach and we cooked fish on it.

6 There were lots of _____ on the flowers in the garden.

7 Look! There's a _____ eating grass in the field.

8 We were very hot when we got to the top of the _____.

9 In winter, the lake had lots of snow and _____ on it.

10 In North America, lots of the trees turn yellow and red in the _____.

4 Put the words from the box into the table.

> autumn   beach   bee   camel   desert   forest   island
> rabbit   spring   summer   winter   wood

animals	seasons	places

Speaking

Listen and answer the questions about the natural world.

40

1 Tell me about your favourite season.

2 Tell me about nature where you live.

3 Are there any natural places people enjoy visiting in your country?

4 Do you think it's important to take care of nature? Why or why not?

Reading

Read the text about the Valdivian Rainforest.

For each question, choose the correct answer.

Valdivian Rainforest

The Valdivian Rainforest is in South America. It's not the largest rainforest in the **(1)** _____, but it is very big. Many different plants **(2)** _____ in the Valdivian Rainforest because of the weather. The Valdivian Rainforest is cooler than most rainforests because there are mountains in parts of it and the weather is colder there. So plants that like colder weather, such as bamboo, grow on the mountains in the rainforest.

There are **(3)** _____ of animals in the rainforest **(4)** _____. It is where the Americas' smallest cat, the kodkod, and the world's smallest deer, the southern pudu both live.

Another thing that makes the Valdivian Rainforest special is that it is the **(5)** _____ rainforest in the world which has glaciers in it. Glaciers are big areas of ice.

1	**A** space	**B** world	**C** nature
2	**A** come	**B** make	**C** grow
3	**A** most	**B** lots	**C** many
4	**A** even	**B** and	**C** too
5	**A** only	**B** another	**C** most

Grammar: Comparatives and superlatives

We use comparatives to compare one thing with another thing.
The Valdivian Rainforest *is cooler than* most rainforests.

We use superlatives to compare something with the whole group that it belongs to.
It is *the* world's *smallest* deer.

Circle the correct words to complete the sentence.
The River Nile is *longer than / the longest* river in the world and it is *more famous than / the most famous* the River Seine in France.

Listening

You will hear a boy, Dylan, talking to his mum about a school project.

41

What is each person in the group finding information about?

People	Activity
1 Emily	**A** mountains
2 Martha	**B** islands
3 Oscar	**C** forests
4 Mia	**D** rivers
5 Dylan	**E** lakes
	F seas
	G explorers

Writing

Write a story.

Look at the pictures.

Write the story shown in the pictures.

Write **35 words** or more. Use these words to help you. Remember to change the verbs to the past.

explorers > lost > forest > suddenly > monkey > take map > after a long time > arrive > hotel > monkey > sitting > swimming pool > eat > banana

writing tip

In Writing Part 7, use some of these words and phrases to connect your ideas: *and, so, but, then, suddenly, after that, after a long time.*

Vocabulary

1 Fill in the words.

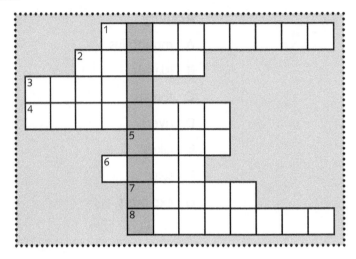

Clues

1

2

3

4

5

6
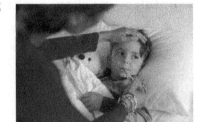

7

8

Find the missing word in blue. Complete the sentence.

You take _____ when you are ill.

2 Look at the photo. Circle the correct words.

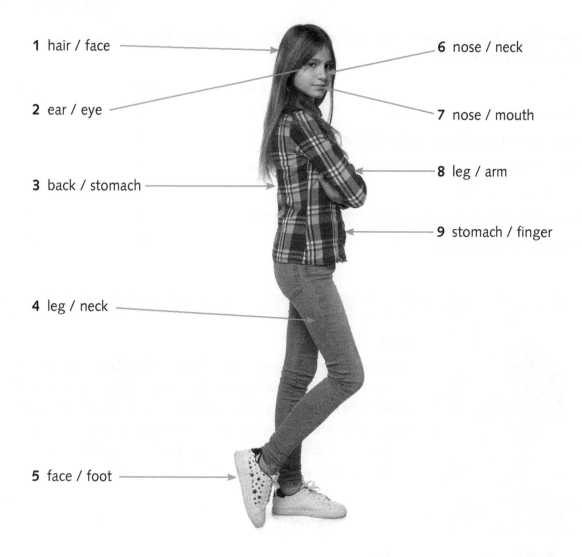

1 hair / face

2 ear / eye

3 back / stomach

4 leg / neck

5 face / foot

6 nose / neck

7 nose / mouth

8 leg / arm

9 stomach / finger

Speaking

 **Look at the pictures that show different exercises.**

42 **Listen and answer the questions.**

1 Which of these different ways of exercising do you like? Why?

2 Do you think doing exercise with other people is more fun than doing it by yourself?

3 Do you prefer running or walking? Why?

4 Do you think it's important to exercise? Why or why not?

Reading

Read the three texts about a school visitor. For each question, choose the correct answer A, B or C.

		Erin	Luke	Jess
1	Who had a class visitor on Thursday?	A	B	C
2	Who was given something by their visitor?	A	B	C
3	Whose class visitor is a friend's parent?	A	B	C
4	Who thinks their visitor is brave?	A	B	C
5	Whose visitor talked about exercise?	A	B	C
6	Who went inside an ambulance?	A	B	C

Our school visitor

Erin

On Monday, a visitor came to talk to my class. She was a dentist. She told us all about our teeth and how to look after them. She explained what a dentist does and why she likes being one. She was very nice and she gave us each a new toothbrush. She showed us how to brush our teeth every morning and every night before we go to bed.

Luke

On Wednesday afternoon, an ambulance driver came to my school. He came in his ambulance. He showed us the ambulance and I went inside, too! It was really interesting. He told us how he has to drive very quickly to get to a sick person and take them to hospital. I think ambulance drivers are very brave. I'd like to be an ambulance driver when I am older.

Jess

On Thursday, my friend Sienna's mum came in to our class. She is a yoga teacher. She came to tell us all about yoga and why it is a good exercise to do. She showed us how to do some yoga. It was fun!

Listening

For each question, choose the correct answer A, B or C.

43 **You will hear a boy, Will, talking to his mum about how he is feeling.**

1 Will has got

   A toothache.

   B stomach ache.

   C a pain in his neck.

2 Mum says Will needs

   A to go to the hospital.

   B to go to bed.

   C to call an ambulance.

3 Mum gives Will

   A some medicine.

   B a toothbrush.

   C some tea.

> **Listening tip**
>
> In Listening Part 3, read the instructions carefully. They will tell you the situation of the conversation. When you know the situation, think about key words you might hear, for example: *You will hear a boy talking to his mum about how he is feeling.*
>
> Words you might hear: *sick, ill, stomach ache, pain, temperature,* etc.
>
> This will help you to know what the speakers are saying more quickly as you listen.

Grammar: Future with *will*

We use *will* to talk about recent decisions and make offers.

I'*ll* phone the doctor. (decision)

I'*ll* get you some medicine. (offer)

Use *will* in a contraction: I will > I'*ll*

Write a sentence about what you will do this evening, using *I'll* …

Writing

Write a text message.

You can't go to school today because you aren't feeling well. Write a text message to your English friend Julie.

Say:

• that you can't come to school today

• what is wrong and why

• what you will do to get better.

Write **25 words** or more.

Unit 1 Clothes and accessories

Speaking

Track 1

Now let's talk about clothes and accessories.

1 What clothes and accessories are you wearing now?
2 What clothes do you wear to school? Do you have to wear a school uniform?
3 What type of clothes do you not like wearing?
4 What do you like wearing in hot weather?
5 Do you ever wear any jewellery?

Listening

Track 2

1 What is Grace wearing to the party this evening?

Mia: Hi Grace, what are you wearing to the party this evening? Are you wearing your new black dress?
Grace: Hi Mia. No, I'm not wearing my new black dress because it's dirty, I might wear my blue dress.
Mia: Oh yes, wear your blue dress – it's lovely. I'm wearing my green skirt with my new grey T-shirt.
Grace: Cool!

2 How much does the red jacket cost?

Alex: Ooh look at this jacket, Kim. I really like it.
Kim: How much is it, Alex?
Alex: It's £12.
Kim: How much money have you got?
Alex: £20.
Kim: Are you going to buy it?
Alex: Maybe! Oh, wait. Look at the red jacket over there.
Kim: That's nice too, but it's more expensive. It's £14.50.
Alex: Hmmm… that's OK. I've got enough money.
Kim: So, you're buying the red jacket?
Alex: Yes, I am.

Unit 2 Food and drink

Vocabulary

Track 3

orange	apple
boiled egg	cheese
pepper	strawberries
meat	jam
tomato	

Speaking

Track 4

Now let's talk about food.

1 Tell me about something you ate yesterday.
2 What do you like to eat for breakfast?
3 What is your favourite food?
4 Do you ever go on picnics? What food do you take with you?
5 Who cooks the meals in your home?

Listening

Track 5

You will hear a waitress talking to a customer about the menu.

Waitress: Hello and welcome to Daisy's Kitchen. Have you been here before?
Customer: No, never.
Waitress: OK, so the menu is on the board. Let me go through it with you. For lunch today we have soup of the day, which is chicken soup. The soup costs £3.50.
Customer: Does it come with bread?
Waitress: Yes, of course. We also have sandwiches. Today's sandwiches are cheese and tomato or egg salad. They cost £3. If you are very hungry, you might prefer our steak and chips, which costs £6, or the fish curry and rice, which costs £6.50.
Customer: Great, thanks. Can I ask, are you open for dinner, too?
Waitress: Yes, we serve breakfast, lunch and dinner. We're open from 8 in the morning until 10 in the evening.

Unit 3 Colours and time

Speaking

Track 6

Now let's talk about colours and time.

1 What's your favourite colour?
2 Describe your hair and your eyes.
3 What different colours are there in your bedroom? Describe the furniture, floor, walls and curtains.
4 What did you do yesterday?
5 What do you like to do at the weekend?
6 What's your favourite month? Why is it your favourite?

Listening

Track 7

1 You will hear a girl, Kate, talking about shopping. Why did Kate buy the jumper?

John: Hi Kate, what did you buy at the shops?
Kate: I bought a new jumper. It's pale pink.
John: Pink? I thought you hated pink! Didn't you want a blue jumper?
Kate: Yes, I did, but the blue jumpers were dark blue and I wanted a pale jumper.

2 You will hear a boy giving directions to his house. What colour is the boy's house?

Hi Niall. So, come to my house on Sunday morning and we can go to football practice together. I live on Whitchurch Road. It's the road with all the colourful houses. It's number 10, you can't miss it – my house is in between a dark blue house and a pink house and it's yellow.

3 You will hear two girls discussing earrings. Which do they like best?

Amy: Ooh, look at these earrings, Farah.
Farah: Ooh, yes – they're lovely.
Amy: Which do you like best?
Farah: I'm not sure… I like the purple ones. What about you?
Amy: I really like the blue ones, but I like the purple ones more. I think they're the nicest. I definitely don't like the pink ones, though. Do you?
Farah: No, not at all.

Unit 4 Family and friends

Speaking

Track 8

Now let's talk about family and friends.

1 Do you have any brothers or sisters?
2 Do you have any cousins?
3 Do you have a small or a large family?
4 Who is your best friend? What do you like to do together?
5 Do you have a pen friend?

Listening

Track 9

You will hear Fred talking to his mother about a family picnic. What will each person bring or do?

Mum: Hey Fred, don't forget the family picnic on Sunday, will you?

Fred: Of course not, Mum. Grandma's coming, isn't she?
Mum: Yes, and we want to make it very special. Can you make a cake for her?
Fred: Oh no, Mum! Can't you just buy a cake at the shops?
Mum: No, you make great cakes.
Fred: Auntie Jane makes great cakes, too. Can't she make a cake?
Mum: No, Auntie Jane's making the salads. And Grandma loves your cakes.
Fred: Well, what about Mabel? What's Mabel doing?
Mum: Mabel's going shopping for all the food.
Fred: I know, I could bring the music.
Mum: No, Cousin John's bringing the music.
Fred: Well, I could bring games to play – like beach tennis, cricket….
Mum: Uncle Mike's bringing games. Please make a cake for your grandma.
Fred: Oh, Mum, can't you make the cake?
Mum: No. I'm bringing Grandma so I haven't got time.
Fred: OK, OK, I'll make the cake.
Mum: Thanks, Fred.

Unit 5 Hobbies and leisure

Speaking

Track 10

Now let's talk about hobbies and leisure.

1 Do you have any hobbies?
2 What hobbies did you have when you were six?
3 What hobby would you like to try?
4 Do you go to any clubs? What clubs do you go to? Who do you go with?
5 Have you ever been on holiday? Where did you go? What did you do?

Listening

Track 11

1 You will hear Jimmy talking to his grandma. What is Grandma's hobby?

Grandma: Hi Jimmy, how are you?
Jimmy: I'm bored.
Grandma: Oh… why?
Jimmy: I'm reading a book, but it's not very interesting.
Grandma: Well, maybe you can do something else?
Jimmy: Hmmm… I haven't really got any hobbies. What are your hobbies, Grandma?

Grandma: Well, I liked dancing when I was young. Now I've got my bike, and I like cycling in the park. Cycling is good for you. Why don't you come with me?

2 You will hear a family trying to decide where to go. Where do they decide to go?

Boy: Mum, Dad, can we go to the beach today?
Dad: But it's cold. Let's go to the museum.
Boy: The museum's boring. Can we go to the park?
Mum: I'd like to go shopping.
Boy: No!
Mum: You can buy a new video game.
Boy: Oh yes! I'd like a new video game.
Dad: And I need some new shoes. Let's go!

3 You will hear two friends talking about their weekend. Where have they just been?

Man: That was awful, wasn't it?
Woman: Yes – I was so cold all weekend.
Man: Me too! The rain came into my tent, so I couldn't sleep. I'm so tired!
Woman: And the food was really bad.
Man: I hate cooking over a fire. The food never cooks properly.
Woman: I'm really hungry.

Unit 6 House and home

Vocabulary

Track 12

| garage | bathroom | bedroom | living room |
| kitchen | roof | garden | office |

Speaking

Track 13

Now let's talk about house and home.

1 Do you live in an apartment or a house?
2 How many rooms are there in your home?
3 What's your favourite room in your home and why?
4 Have you got a garden?
5 Describe your perfect home.

Listening

Track 14

1 What does Paul need to buy for his bedroom?

Aunt: OK, Paul. What do we need to buy for your bedroom? Ooh… look at these lovely lamps! Do you need a new lamp?
Paul: Thanks, Auntie Jane, but I've got a lamp. I do need a new bin to go under my desk though.
Aunt: OK. Let's look at those bins over there.

2 What wouldn't Emma have in her perfect house?

Emma: In my perfect house, I would have a big living room with large windows. I wouldn't have a sofa, I'd have a big armchair and a bookcase next to the window. I'd sit and read books and look out of the window.

Unit 7 Places: Buildings

Speaking

Track 15

Now let's talk about buildings.

1 Are the buildings where you live modern or old?
2 What's the biggest building where you live?
3 Do you prefer to go to a museum or a sports centre? Why?
4 Have you ever been to the theatre?
5 How often do you go to the cinema? Who do you go with?

Listening

Track 16

You will hear Ava talking to her friend, Sam, about a day out.

Sam: Hi Ava, what did you do this weekend?
Ava: Actually, I had a day out.
Sam: Really? Did you go to the museum? I know you wanted to see the paintings there.
Ava: I wanted to go to the museum, but the bus was late, so I went to the library instead.
Sam: The library next to the King's Hotel?
Ava: No, the other library, next to the shopping centre.
Sam: Oh! Was it boring?
Ava: Usually I don't really like libraries – they're too quiet – but this library is really cool. It was built three years ago and it's very big and modern and really beautiful. And it's got a great café inside.

Unit 8 Sport

Speaking

Track 17

Now let's talk about sport.

1 What sports do you like? Is there a sport you don't like?
2 Is there a sport you play every week?
3 Are you a member of any sports clubs or teams?
4 Have you ever entered a sports competition?
5 Is there a sport you would like to try?

Listening

Track 18

You will hear a volleyball coach talking to her team.

OK, team! Please listen. I'm going to give you the information you need about next week's volleyball competition. The competition's on Wednesday next week and it's going to be at Whitehawk School, so we will need to travel there by bus. The competition starts at four o'clock, so we will leave school at quarter past three. Please remember to wear your volleyball kit to school on that day and bring water and a snack with you. Are there any questions?

Unit 9 Documents and texts

Speaking

Track 19

Now let's talk about documents and texts.

1 Do you read comics? Did you read comics when you were younger?
2 What book are you reading? Are you enjoying it?
3 When do you send cards? Who do you send them to?
4 Can you tell me about a project you did at school?
5 How often do your parents read newspapers?

Listening

Track 20

1 **You will hear a girl, Patty, talking to her teacher about learning French. What does her teacher say she should do?**

Patty: Hi Mr Brown. Can you help me please? I can't do my French homework. I don't understand. I think my French is very bad.
Mr Brown: Don't worry, Patty, it's very hard to learn a language.
Patty: Yes, it is. Do you think I should buy another textbook and study more?
Mr Brown: Studying is very important, but actually I think you should listen to things in French and that will help a lot.
Patty: Do you mean listen to French music?
Mr Brown: No. I mean that you should watch French films. That will really help you.

2 **You will hear a boy and his mum. What has the boy forgotten to bring?**

Mum: Come on, Harry. We need to go.
Harry: OK, Mum. I'm ready.
Mum: Good, have you got everything?

Harry: Yes! I've got my water bottle, my sunglasses, my hat, my notebook and my pen.
Mum: Great. Can you text Rebecca and tell her we will be there in fifteen minutes please?
Harry: Oh no! I haven't got my phone. Can I use yours?

3 **You will hear a teacher telling the class about a school trip. What is he asking parents to do?**

OK class 6T. The school trip to the science museum is next Thursday. I've sent your parents an email. You must ask your parents to read the email before the trip. The email tells them how to complete the online form. They must complete the form if you want to go on the trip. When your parents have completed the form, I will send them a text message.

Unit 10 Communication and technology

Speaking

Track 21

Now let's talk about communication and technology.

1 What types of technology do you use every day?
2 Do you chat online with friends? What do you chat about?
3 Do you like taking photographs? What do you use to take them?
4 What websites do you like best?
5 What do you like doing on the internet?

Listening

Track 22

You will hear a teacher talking to the class about computer club.

Hello everyone! I'm going to tell you about an exciting new school club called computer club. It's for everyone and you don't need to know anything about computers – we'll teach you. I'm going to give you some information about the club, which will take place in the Computer Room 'A' twenty-three. The club will be on Tuesdays and it will start on the second of April and finish on the seventeenth of June. Now the times of the club: It will start at four p.m. and finish at half past five. You have to pay for the club. It costs three pounds each week. You'll learn lots of useful things like how to write an email, print photos and make your own website. So, if you're interested, you need to ask your parents to send an email to Mrs Brown. Here's her address on the board. I hope you can come! Are there any questions?

Unit 11 Education

Speaking

Track 23

Now let's talk about education.

1 What's your favourite subject at school?
2 Is there a subject you don't like?
3 How many English lessons do you have each week?
4 How many hours of homework do you have each week?
5 Where and when do you prefer to do your homework?

Listening

Track 24

You will hear a teacher talking about a student.

Teacher: Hello Mr Thomas. How are you?

Mr Thomas: I'm very well, thank you.

Teacher: Good. Let's talk about your daughter, Lottie. Lottie's a lovely student. She tries very hard. She's very advanced in English and maths.

Mr Thomas: Great!

Teacher: Yes, she always wants to learn in class, and she usually does all her homework.

Mr Thomas: Fantastic!

Teacher: Yes, but last week she didn't. The class were doing a science project and I asked them to do some research and make notes at home. But Lottie didn't do anything. I had to give her a low mark for the project.

Mr Thomas: Oh, I see… I think I know why Lottie didn't do the homework.

Teacher: Yes?

Mr Thomas: Our computer broke last week.

Unit 12 Entertainment and media

Speaking

Track 25

Now let's talk about entertainment. Look at the photos.

1 Which of these types of entertainment do you like? Why?
2 Which of these types of entertainment don't you like? Why not?
3 Which is more fun, watching a show or being in a show? Why?

4 Do you prefer going out or staying at home for entertainment? Why?

Listening

Track 26

You will hear Lily talking to her dad about the weekend. What is she doing with each of her friends?

Dad: Hey Lily, have you got any plans for this weekend?

Lily: Yes, I have. I'm very busy. I'm going to see all my friends.

Dad: Are you all going out together?

Lily: Oh no. I'm doing different things with different people. I'm going to Jane's house on Friday evening and we're going to eat pizza and listen to music. Then on Saturday morning, I'm going to go to Zack's house and we're going to practise drums for the school concert.

Dad: Doesn't Billy play drums too? Is he going to practise at Zack's house with you?

Lily: No, he isn't. But on Saturday afternoon, I'm going to Billy's house and we're going to play chess. Then on Sunday, Rebecca is coming to our house and we're going to play my new video game.

Dad: Which one?

Lily: It's called Dancing Queens.

Dad: Right. And what are you going to do on Sunday afternoon?

Lily: On Sunday afternoon I'm going to see Issy.

Dad: Are you going to go to the dance show at the Thirsk centre?

Lily: No, we're not going to go to the dance show, we're going to play a board game.

Dad: Wow! You're right, you're very busy, Lily.

Unit 13 Personal feelings, opinions and experiences

Speaking

Track 27

Now let's talk about personal feelings, opinions and experiences.

1 What makes you happy?
2 What are you afraid of?
3 What is the most interesting thing you have done?
4 Would you like to be famous? Why or why not?
5 Can you tell me about a time when you were lucky?

Listening
Track 28

You will hear a girl, Mona, talking to her friend Jay about a person she met.

Jay: Hi Mona. You're late for art club.

Mona: Sorry, I met this person on my way here.

Jay: Oh! Who? Was it someone famous?

Mona: No, it wasn't. It was a painter. She was painting a picture on the wall of a building in town.

Jay: Oh! Was it very bad?

Mona: No, it was amazing. She's a brilliant painter.

Jay: What was the painting of?

Mona: It was of a group of young people dancing.

Jay: That's interesting.

Mona: Yes, but some old people didn't like it. They weren't very pleasant to the painter.

Jay: Oh dear!

Unit 14 Places: Countryside

Speaking
Track 29

Now let's talk about the countryside. Look at the photos.

1 Which of these places do you like best? Why?
2 Which of these places don't you like? Why not?
3 What different activities can you do in each of these places? Which do you think are the most fun?
4 Where would you prefer to go on holiday? Why?

Listening
Track 30

1 Where is Gill's cousin working now?

Man: Gill, guess who I saw yesterday in the museum shop! Your cousin – you know, the one who was working at that campsite in the countryside last summer.

Woman: Tom? At the museum? That's impossible!

Man: Why?

Woman: Well, he's working in a post office in a small village in Scotland now. He hardly ever comes home.

2 Where are they going to have a picnic?

Man: Oh no! Look! Black clouds. It's going to rain.

Woman: That's a pity. Well, we can't have a picnic at the beach in this weather.

Man: Shall we go to the lake? We can sit under the trees.

Woman: That's too far. Shall we go to the park? Then we can come home if it rains too much.

Man: Great! Shall I make some sandwiches?

Unit 15 Travel and transport

Speaking
Track 31

Now let's talk about travel and transport.

1 How do you travel to school?
2 What transport do you not like using?
3 Have you ever travelled by train or plane? Where did you go?
4 Do many visitors come to your country?
5 Would you like to be an explorer? Why or why not?

Listening
Track 32

1 You will hear a teacher talking about a school trip. What time will the class leave?

There is a problem with the trains on the underground so we will now go by bus. The journey will take longer now. It'll take one and a half hours, so we have to leave at half past seven in the morning and not eight o'clock. Please meet at the bus stop.

2 You will hear a man and a woman on a car journey. Where do they decide to stop?

Man: There's a lot of traffic on this motorway. I'm tired. Shall we stop for a while?

Woman: Good idea! I'd like a drink.

Man: Is there a petrol station near here?

Woman: Let me look on the map… No, there isn't. It's quite a long way to the next one.

Man: Oh no!

Woman: But there's a town in about five kilometres. We could stop there.

Man: OK, let's stop there.

Woman: Wait! What's that sign?

Man: Oh yes, it says there's a supermarket in two kilometres.

Woman: And it's got a café.

Man: Great! Let's stop there.

3 You will hear a father talking to his children. How will they travel to the festival?

OK, I'm looking online and I can see that there are lots of trains to the music festival, and there are lots of buses too. Wait! Oh, there's a problem with the trains next week and the buses don't stop at the festival. So, we'll have to go by car instead. What a shame! I love travelling by train.

Unit 16 Work and jobs

Speaking

Track 33

Now let's talk about work and jobs.

1 What jobs do some of the people in your family have?
2 What do you think is the best job? Why?
3 What do you think is the worst job? Why?
4 Is working in an office a good job?
5 Where is a good place to work? Why?

Listening

Track 34

You will hear a teacher telling her class about a job.

Good morning class. Please listen. I want to tell you something very exciting. A film company is looking for two children to be actors in a film. Both children must be between seven and ten years old. They must have brown hair. And each child actor will earn thirty pounds. Please see me after the class if you are interested.

Unit 17 Places: Town and city

Speaking

Track 35

Now let's talk about about towns and cities.

1 Do you live in a town or city?
2 What is your favourite place to go in a city? Why?
3 Is there a bus station where you live? Is there a railway station or an airport?
4 How often do you go to a park or a playground?
5 Tell me something about the street where you live.

Listening

Track 36

You will hear a boy, Lewis, talking to his mum about his school trip. Where did the people in his class want to go?

Mum: Hi Lewis, how was your school trip today?
Boy: Well... it was OK, but everyone wanted to go to different places.
Mum: Oh no!
Boy: Yes. First, we took the underground to the city centre and visited the museum. Then we had time to go to one more place after lunch.
Mum: Did Mr Philips let the class choose where?
Boy: Yes.
Mum: Did you choose the zoo, Lewis?

Boy: No, I didn't. Isaac chose the zoo. I wanted to go to the park because it was a lovely day and there's a big lake there and you can go on a boat.
Mum: Oh yes, that's nice. And there's a playground, isn't there?
Boy: Yes, Dina wanted to go to the playground.
Mum: Where did Jay want to go?
Boy: He wanted to go to the railway station because he loves trains.
Mum: It is a very interesting railway station because it's very old. I think there's a beautiful bridge there too.
Boy: Well, Jay didn't want to see the bridge, he only wanted to see the railway station.
Mum: What about Mr Philips?
Boy: Mr Philips wanted us all to go and visit the market. After a long time, we couldn't decide where to go, so we went to the market. It was really boring!
Mum: Oh dear!

Unit 18 Weather and months

Speaking

Track 37

Now let's talk about weather and months.

1 What is the weather like today?
2 What is your favourite weather? Why? What do you like to do in this weather?
3 What month is your birthday?
4 Which is your favourite month? Why?
5 How often does it snow where you live?

Listening

Track 38

1 When is the man getting married?

Woman: Congratulations, darling! I'm so happy for you! When's the big day?
Man: We were thinking of July next year. On the thirtieth, because it's our anniversary. We met on the thirtieth.
Woman: But Seville is too hot in July!
Man: Yes, I know! We can't manage June so we decided May. May the third.

2 Why can't the man and woman go out?

Man: Look how foggy it is outside! We can't go out in this weather.
Woman: Oh dear. Well, there's a bit of wind so maybe the fog will clear up.
Man: Let's wait and see.
Woman: All right. Would you like a cup of tea?

Unit 19 The natural world

Vocabulary

Track 39

lake	forest
mountain	grass
sky	tree

Speaking

Track 40

Now let's talk about the natural world.

1 Tell me about your favourite season.
2 Tell me about nature where you live.
3 Are there any natural places people enjoy visiting in your country?
4 Do you think it's important to take care of nature? Why or why not?

Listening

Track 41

You will hear a boy, Dylan, talking to his mum about a school project. What is each person in the group finding information about?

Dylan: Hi, Mum.
Mum: Hi, Dylan.
Dylan: I've got homework to do tonight for a school project.
Mum: What's it about?
Dylan: The natural world. We're making a poster and each person has to find out information about one thing.
Mum: Oh, that sounds interesting. What have you decided?
Dylan: Well… Emily wants to find out information about forests because she has been to the Amazon rainforest and she's got lots of photos.
Mum: Is she writing about the Amazon River as well?
Dylan: No, I don't think so. Martha wants to find out about mountains because she has been to Mount Kilimanjaro in Africa.
Mum: But what will you do? What about different seas?
Dylan: Hmm… I don't think I want to learn about water because Oscar is finding out about rivers and Mia is finding out about lakes. I don't know what to do.
Mum: I know. You could learn about islands. You liked exploring that island on holiday last year.
Dylan: Yes, you're right. I did. But I really like exploring. I could find out information about explorers! Yes, that's what I will do.

Unit 20 Health, medicine and exercise

Speaking

Track 42

Now let's talk about exercise. Look at the pictures.

1 Which of these different ways of exercising do you like? Why?
2 Do you think doing exercise with other people is more fun than doing it by yourself?
3 Do you prefer running or walking? Why?
4 Do you think it's important to exercise? Why or why not?

Listening

Track 43

You will hear a boy, Will, talking to his mum about how he is feeling.

Will: Mum, I don't feel well.
Mum: Oh no! Is your head hot?
Will: Yes, it is and it hurts.
Mum: Does it hurt anywhere else?
Will: I've got a pain in my neck.
Mum: I think you've got a temperature. Have you got a stomach ache?
Will: No, I haven't.
Mum: Are you tired?
Will: Yes, I am. I'm very tired.
Mum: Oh dear!
Will: Do I need to go to the hospital? Shall we call an ambulance?
Mum: No, I don't think you need an ambulance or to go to the hospital. But I will phone the doctor in the morning.
Will: OK.
Mum: Here is some medicine… I'll get you a drink. Would you like tea or water?
Will: Water, please.
Mum: OK. And then you must brush your teeth and go to bed.
Will: OK. Thanks, Mum.

Unit 1 Clothes and accessories

Vocabulary

1 1 belt 2 earrings 3 bracelet 4 gloves 5 blouse 6 umbrella

2 She's not wearing: 2, 4, 6, 7, 9, 10

3 B

Grammar Box

Sample answer: The boy's / He's wearing trainers, jeans and a shirt, but he isn't wearing any socks or sunglasses.

Speaking

Suggested answers:

1 I'm wearing a red skirt, a white T-shirt and a big blue jumper. I'm also wearing earrings.

2 Yes, I have to wear a uniform to school. It's a blue dress and white socks and black shoes.

3 I don't like wearing hats and scarves in the winter. They're too hot.

4 In hot weather I like wearing shorts, and when it's sunny I wear a hat. I don't like wearing sunglasses.

5 Yes, I usually wear a bracelet and I sometimes wear a watch.

Reading

1 A

2 B

3 C

Listening

1 B

2 A

Grammar Box

Sample answer: This weekend I'm riding my horse, tidying my bedroom and meeting my friend in the park.

Writing

Sample answer:

Hi Freddy,

Thalia's having a party on Saturday at 4.30 pm and she's inviting you. It's at her house – number 53 Osborne Road. I'm wearing my new white jeans and red shirt. What are you wearing?

Max

Unit 2 Food and drink

Vocabulary

1 1 pepper 2 boiled egg 3 tomato 4 jam 5 orange 6 apple 7 strawberries 8 cheese 9 meat

2 fork, glass, knife, plate, spoon

3 1 snack 2 chef 3 barbecue 4 fridge 5 breakfast 6 picnic 7 dinner 8 kitchen 9 lunch 10 café

Speaking

Suggested answers:

1 Yesterday I ate spaghetti with tomato sauce and peas for dinner. It was delicious!

2 I like to eat yogurt with fruit for breakfast. I really like strawberries and bananas.

3 My favourite food is pizza.

4 Yes, I go on picnics in the summer. I like going to the beach for a picnic. I take bread and cheese and tomatoes.

5 My mum usually cooks the meals in my home. Sometimes my sister cooks too. She's 15.

Reading

1 B

2 B

3 A

Grammar Box

Sample answer: Yes, I've eaten something different. I've eaten snake.

Listening

1 chicken

2 tomato

3 3

4 Steak

5 6

6 Curry

7 10

Writing

Sample answer:

Lucy,

I want to cook a special dinner for Mum and Dad tonight. I've decided to cook fish and chips. I need to go to the supermarket and get some fish, some potatoes and some salad. Will you come with me?

Tom

Unit 3 Colours and time

Vocabulary

1 1 black c 2 green e 3 orange a 4 brown b
   5 purple f 6 yellow d 7 pink h 8 red i
   9 silver j 10 blue g

2 1 morning 2 afternoon 3 winter 4 months
   5 midnight 6 noon 7 spring 8 days
   9 Tomorrow 10 Yesterday

3 1 golden 2 dark 3 pale 4 white

Speaking

Suggested answers:

1 My favourite colour is purple.

2 I've got dark brown hair and green eyes.

3 My bedroom is white. I have a blue and white curtains and an orange carpet.
   My bed and my wardrobe are also white.

4 Yesterday I went to the beach because it was Sunday.

5 At the weekend, I like to watch TV and play video games with my sister. Sometimes I like to go to the beach with my family or friends.

6 My favourite month is September because it's my birthday in September.

Reading

1 C 2 A 3 B 4 A 5 C

Grammar Box

Sample answer: Orange is made by mixing yellow and red.

Listening

1 C

2 C

3 A

Writing

Sample answer:

Hi Poppy,

I get up at 6.30 am and I get the bus to school at 7.30 am. School is from 8.00 in the morning to 3.30 in the afternoon. I usually go swimming after school and get home at about 5.00.
In the evening, I have dinner, do my homework and watch TV.

Jilly

Unit 4 Family and friends

Vocabulary

1 1 wife 2 aunt 3 brother 4 parents
   5 grandparents 6 husband 7 children
   8 sister 9 cousin 10 granddaughter
   11 grandson 12 uncle 13 daughter
   14 son 15 grandchildren

Grammar Box

Sample answer: Aunt Lily is my mother's sister.

2 1 group 2 married 3 wife 4 husband
   5 guests

Speaking

Suggested answers:

1 Yes, I've got two brothers and one sister.

2 No, I haven't got any cousins. I have got an uncle, but he doesn't have children.

3 I have a large family. There is me, my two brothers, my sister, my mum and dad, my mum's sister and my grandparents.

4 My best friend is Michael. We like playing football and going cycling together.

5 No, I haven't got a pen friend but I would like to have one.

Reading

1 for 2 any 3 my 4 got 5 than 6 are

Listening

1 F 2 B 3 D 4 E 5 A

Writing

Sample answer:

A family, a mum, a dad, their son and their baby are going for a walk in the park.

Unit 5 Hobbies and leisure

Vocabulary

1 Across: 1 barbecue 4 camera 7 campsite 9 magazine

Down: 1 beach 2 bicycle 3 park 5 museum 6 video game 8 picnic

2 1 musician 2 competition 3 barbecue 4 camp 5 photos

3 1 ride 2 go to 3 play 4 go 5 go 6 listen to; play 7 take; have 8 have 9 go to 10 go 11 join; go to 12 take

Speaking

Suggested answers:

1 Yes, I do. I like playing the guitar and singing.

2 When I was six, my hobby was dancing.

3 I'd like to try horse riding.

4 Yes, I do. I go to comic club on Wednesdays. We draw comics there. I go with my friend Ailsa.

5 Yes, I have been on holiday. I went to France. I went swimming in the sea and had picnics on the beach.

Reading

1 A 2 C 3 C

Listening

1 C 2 B 3 A

Grammar Box

Sample answer: I go swimming every evening. Swimming is good exercise.

Writing

Sample answer:

Hi Oliver,

What would you like to do on Saturday? Would you like to come to my house and play video games? Can you come at 3.30?

Henry

Unit 6 House and home

Vocabulary

1 1 roof 2 office 3 bedroom 4 bathroom 5 garden 6 living room 7 kitchen 8 garage

2 1 False: It's a house.
2 True
3 True: There is a table and two chairs outside.
4 False: The fridge is in the kitchen.
5 False
6 False: There is only one toilet.
7 True
8 False
9 True
10 False

3 1 sink 2 address 3 rubbish 4 curtains 5 lights 6 drawer 7 key 8 blanket

Speaking

Suggested answers:

1 I live in an apartment.

2 There are seven rooms in my home. There's a kitchen, a living room, a bathroom and four bedrooms.

3 My favourite room is my bedroom because it's pink and pretty.

4 No, I haven't got a garden but I live near to the park.

5 My perfect home would have a swimming pool and a cinema.

Reading

1 from 2 play 3 are 4 His 5 when 6 What

Grammar Box

Sample answer: This is my desk and these are my English books.

Listening

1 C

2 A

Writing

Sample answer:

Hi Luke,

I'd like to invite you to see my new apartment. Would you like to come on Wednesday after school at 4 pm? My address is 11 Spring Road.

Eddie

Unit 7 Places: Buildings

Vocabulary

1 1 bank 2 café 3 castle 4 cinema 5 factory 6 hospital 7 hotel 8 library 9 museum 10 pharmacy 11 school 12 theatre

2 1 B 2 D 3 F 4 G 5 J 6 A 7 E 8 I 9 C 10 H

Tip: A 'garage' can be where you park your car at home like you learned in Unit 6 and can also be where you go to get your car fixed.

Speaking

Suggested answers:

1 There are a lot of modern buildings where I live.

2 The biggest building is the museum.

3 I prefer to go to the sports centre because I like doing sports.

4 No, I've never been to the theatre, but I would like to go.

5 I go to the cinema once a month. I go with my family.

Reading

1 B

2 B

3 A

Grammar Box

was; built

Sample answer: My apartment was built thirty years ago / in the 1990s / a long time ago.

Listening

1 B

2 B

3 A

Writing

Sample answer:

Hi Aunt Pauline and Uncle David,

I'm very excited you are coming to visit next month. You should visit the royal palace. It's very old and very interesting. The queen lives there and sometimes you can see her in the garden.

May

Unit 8 Sport

Vocabulary

1 1 surfing 2 volleyball 3 rugby 4 badminton 5 fishing 6 hockey 7 basketball 8 windsurfing 9 tennis 10 riding 11 table tennis

Words in blue: sports centre.

2 go: swimming, fishing, cycling, skiing, windsurfing, walking

play: volleyball, baseball, table tennis, football, badminton, hockey

3 1 member 2 club 3 practise 4 coach 5 bat 6 kit 7 team 8 throws 9 hits 10 catch

Grammar Box

1 B

2 A

Speaking

Suggested answers:

1 I like badminton, and I love football. I don't like swimming.

2 Yes, there is. I play football every Saturday.

3 Yes, I am. I'm a member of the football team.

4 Yes, I have. I've entered lots of football competitions with my team. We're very good.

5 Yes, there is. I'd like to try tennis.

Reading

1 B

2 A

3 C

4 A

5 A

6 C

Listening

1 Wednesday

2 School

3 bus

4 3.15

5 snack

Writing

Sample answer:

Hi Matt,

There's a new sports club at school. Do you want to come with me? It's a table tennis club and it's on Tuesdays at 4.00 in the sports hall.

Jim

Unit 9 Documents and texts

Vocabulary

1 1 book b
2 newspaper f
3 comic a
4 menu h
5 diary c
6 card g
7 email i
8 letter e
9 magazine d

2 1 licence 2 bill 3 postcard 4 textbooks
5 ticket 6 notebooks 7 form 8 project
9 text 10 advertisement 11 passports
12 message

3 1, 4, 5, 7, 8

Speaking

Suggested answers:

1 No, I don't read comics. I think they're boring. Yes, I did read comics when I was younger – about five years old.

2 I'm reading Harry Potter. Yes, I'm enjoying it. It's very strange and interesting.

3 I send a card to my grandmother for her birthday.

4 I did a project about sport. I made a poster about horse riding.

5 My parents never read newspapers.

Reading

1 B

2 A

3 C

4 A

5 A

Listening

1 C

2 C

3 A

Grammar Box

Sample answer: At this school you should bring lunch from home because the school canteen is not very good, and you must put your phone in your bag in lessons.

Writing

Sample answer:

Hi Lulu,

Can you meet me at my house tomorrow at 11 a.m.? We can go together by bus to my grandparents' house. The bus tickets cost £2.

Jack

Unit 10 Communication and technology

Vocabulary

1 Across: 3 screen 4 computer 7 mouse
8 keyboard 9 laptop

Down: 1 mobile 2 internet 4 camera
5 printer 6 photographs

2 1c 2h 3a 4f 5g 6b 7i 8j 9d 10e

3 1 envelope 2 video game 3 email
4 photography 5 password 6 information
7 website 8 call

Speaking

Suggested answers:

1 I use my phone, my computer and my camera on my phone.

2 I chat online with my friends about school and sport.

3 Yes, I like taking photos and I always use my phone to take photos.

4 I like websites about fashion and I like to watch videos.

5 I like to download music from the internet and I like to surf the internet. I also like to play games online.

Reading

1 1 B 2 A 3 B 4 C 5 C 6 B

Grammar

I decided *to draw* a picture *using* a drawing app on my tablet.

Listening

1 Tuesdays

2 17

3 5.30

4 3

5 Brown

Writing

Sample answer:

Hi Mark,

Can you come shopping with me on Saturday? I want to buy a new tablet. My mum and dad will drive us the shops.

Ted

Unit 11 Education

Vocabulary

1 1 classroom 2 desk 3 ruler 4 student
5 teacher 6 university

2 1 maths 2 geography 3 history

3 1 university 2 exam 3 class 4 homework
5 subject 6 classmate 7 pupil 8 diploma
9 lesson 10 term 11 beginner 12 advanced

Speaking

Suggested answers:

1 My favourite subject at school is English.

2 I don't really like geography.

3 I have three English lessons a week – on Monday, Wednesday and Friday.

4 I have about three hours of homework each week.

5 I prefer to do my homework in the library at school. I like to do it after school. There's an after-school homework club.

Reading

1 B

2 B

3 A

Grammar Box

Sample answer: five; always

Listening

1 C

2 B

3 A

Writing

Sample answer:

Hi Peter,

Tomorrow we've got English, history and science lessons at school. Our teachers are Mr Green for English and Miss Wright for history and science. We usually get homework every day.

Carl

Unit 12 Entertainment and media

Vocabulary

1 1 cartoon 2 television 3 radio 4 festival 5 chess 6 exhibition 7 concert 8 board game 9 laugh

Word in blue: classical

2 drum, keyboard, guitar

3 1 painter 2 singer 3 actor 4 musician 5 dancer 6 photographer

Speaking

Suggested answers:

1 I like drawing and I like going to art exhibitions. I like playing video games too.

2 I don't really like dancing or dance shows. This looks like hip hop and I don't like hip hop. I also don't like rock music or rock music concerts. They are too loud.

3 I think it's more fun to be in a show because it's nice to do something with a group of people.

4 I prefer to stay at home for entertainment because it is nice to be at home. I like listening to music in my bedroom and drawing or painting.

Reading

1 C

2 A

3 C

Grammar Box

Sample answer: This week I'm going to visit my grandparents.

Listening

1 G

2 E

3 B

4 D

5 F

Writing

Sample answer:

Hi Sid,

Would you like to come to a concert with me and my family? It's a classical music concert. It's on Saturday afternoon in the town hall.

Jake

Unit 13 Personal feelings, opinions and experiences

Vocabulary

1

t	y	r	h	a	p	p	y	q	o
b	u	r	u	n	h	a	p	y	
o	n	l	n	o	i	b	o	s	t
r	g	o	g	y	n	o	i	s	y
e	q	z	r	s	p	l	l	r	o
d	m	r	y	e	d	d	y	b	d
t	y	y	e	s	t	r	o	n	g
t	i	r	e	d	g	z	u	n	n
u	a	n	g	r	y	g	n	d	u
q	m	k	t	z	a	n	g	r	i

1 angry 2 tired 3 strong 4 happy 5 bored
6 noisy 7 hungry 8 old 9 young

2 1 difficult 2 soft 3 quiet 4 interested
5 alone 6 sorry 7 famous 8 busy 9 free
10 afraid

3 1c 2a 3e 4b 5f 6d

Speaking

Suggested answers:

1 My dog makes me happy.

2 I'm afraid of spiders.

3 The most interesting thing I have done is going to London with my family.

4 I would like to be famous because I would be rich.

5 I won a prize at school for my painting. I got a notebook!

Reading

1 with

2 the

3 so

4 than

5 because

Grammar Box

Sample answer: It *was raining* and the birds *were singing*. I *was walking* home when I *saw* my friend John.

Listening

1 A

2 C

3 C

Writing

Sample answer:

Hi Ava,

I don't feel well. I have a headache and I'm very tired. I'm sorry but I can't come to your house. Let's meet tomorrow.

Holly

Unit 14 Places: Countryside

Vocabulary

1 1 village d 2 river f 3 railway a 4 lake i
5 mountain b 6 island h 7 forest c
8 campsite e 9 beach j 10 sky g

2 1 forest 2 wood 3 path 4 area 5 rainforest
6 field

3 2, 3, 4, 8, 9, 10, 11

Speaking

Suggested answers:

1 I like the mountains because the air is clean and the views are amazing.

2 I don't like the village. I think it is boring.

3 You can swim at the beach and in the river. You can walk in the forest and in the mountains. I think the beach is most fun.

4 I prefer going on holiday to the beach with my family because the weather is usually sunny.

Reading

1 C

2 B

3 A

4 B

5 A

6 B

Listening

1 C

2 A

Grammar Box

1 It's hot. *Shall I* open a window for you?

2 It's a lovely day. *Shall we* go to the park?

Writing

Sample answer:

Hi Kate,

I went to the countryside at the weekend. I went with my cousin Sofia. We went to the mountains and we went skiing. It was fantastic!

Ursula

Unit 15 Travel and transport

Vocabulary

1 Across: 1 taxi 4 ambulance 5 motorbike 7 boat 8 coach 10 car

Down: 2 aeroplane 3 helicopter 6 tram 9 ship

A ship is bigger than a boat.

2 1 driver 2 pilot 3 explorer 4 mechanic 5 tour guide 6 passenger

3 1 traffic lights 2 tyre 3 roundabout 4 platform 5 motorway 6 suitcase

Speaking

Suggested answers:

1 I walk to school.

2 I don't like buses.

3 Yes, I have. I went by plane to France.

4 Yes, they do. My country is very popular for holidays.

5 No, I wouldn't like to be an explorer because it would be a hard job.

Reading

1 C

2 B

Grammar Box

1 e

2 d

3 b

4 c

5 a

Listening

1 B

2 A

3 A

Grammar Box

1 Yes, I am. / No, I'm not.

2 Yes, I am. / No, I'm not.

3 Yes, it is. / No, it isn't.

4 Yes, it is. / No, it isn't.

Writing

Sample answer:

Hi Milo,

I'll come to visit you on Saturday. I'll travel by train. The train arrives at 4.15 pm at Dusseldorf train station on platform 8. Please can you meet me?

Thanks

Ben

Unit 16 Work and jobs

Vocabulary

1 1 football player
2 teacher
3 tennis player
4 doctor
5 cook
6 waiter
7 singer
8 farmer

9 police officer
10 dentist
11 cleaner
12 artist

2 1 an office
2 businesswoman
3 desk
4 emails
5 meetings
6 a uniform
7 a shop
8 shop assistant
9 uniform
10 customers
11 works
12 photographer

Speaking

Suggested answers:

1 My mum is a doctor and my dad is a manager.

2 I think the best job is being a singer because you are famous.

3 I think being a dentist is the worst job because you have to look into people's mouths.

4 I think working in an office is a good job.

5 A good place to work is the countryside because there is fresh air.

Reading

1 C

2 A

3 B

Grammar Box

Sample answers:

My father liked football. My mother painted pictures.

My father didn't like singing. My mother didn't play a musical instrument.

Listening

1 actor

2 two

3 10

4 brown

5 30

Writing

Sample answer:

There is a woman and she is working on the computer. She's is sitting at a desk, but her baby, son and dog want her to stop working.

Unit 17 Places: Town and city

Vocabulary

1

l	o	b	t	r	h	s	w	m	a
a	i	r	p	o	r	t	n	a	a
s	s	i	k	a	i	a	m	r	a
q	u	d	e	d	t	t	e	k	e
u	g	g	l	k	h	i	e	e	p
a	o	e	r	p	o	o	v	t	b
r	p	r	i	f	e	n	k	g	o
e	c	a	r	p	a	r	k	j	x
p	l	a	y	g	r	o	u	n	d
c	c	d	f	r	a	c	x	p	y

1 car park 2 market 3 bridge 4 playground
5 airport 6 road 7 square 8 station

2 1 C
2 A
3 E
4 D
5 B

3 1 city centre
2 town
3 bus station
4 corner
5 roundabout
6 underground
7 motorway

Speaking

Suggested answers:

1 I live in a town. / I don't live in a town or a city. I live in a village.

2 My favourite place in a city is the city centre because I like shopping.

3 Yes, there is a bus station / railway station / an airport where I live. / No there isn't a bus station / a railway station / an airport (where I live).

4 I go to the park every day because I walk my dog.

5 I live on a long street with lots of houses. There is a park at the end of the street.

Reading

1 B

2 A

3 C

4 A

5 A

Grammar Box

two; first

Listening

1 D

2 E

3 G

4 A

5 F

Writing

Sample answer:

Hi Sara

I'm going to the city centre tomorrow.
I'm going by bus and will arrive at 12.30.
I'm going to the market next to the shops.

Would you like to come?

Karim

Unit 18 Weather and months

Vocabulary

1 Across: 3 rain 5 thunderstorm 7 cloudy
8 snow

Down: 1 windy 2 hot 4 foggy 6 sunny
7 cold

2 1 January
2 February
3 April
4 June
5 August
6 September
7 October
8 December

3 1 March
2 May
3 July
4 November

4 1 cold
2 snow
3 white
4 ice
5 weather
6 snowboarding

Grammar box

Sample answer:

I like the yellow boots. The boots are yellow.

Speaking

Suggested answers:

1 Today it is sunny.

2 My favourite weather is snow because I love skiing.

3 My birthday is in November.

4 My favourite month is May because it's sunny every day.

5 It never snows where I live.

Reading

1 your

2 Is

3 until

4 in

5 me

Grammar Box

It's a *nice, sunny* day.

Listening

1 A

2 B

Writing

Sample answer:

Hi James,

Let's go for a walk in the forest on Saturday. The weather will be hot and sunny, so you should bring a hat and some sunglasses.

See you on Saturday.

Johnny

Unit 19 The natural world

Vocabulary

1 1 mountain
2 lake
3 sky
4 forest
5 grass
6 tree

2 1 north
2 west
3 east
4 south

3 1 grow
2 moon, stars / stars, moon
3 wool
4 desert
5 fire
6 bees
7 rabbit
8 hill
9 ice
10 autumn

4 Animals: bee, camel, rabbit
Seasons: autumn, spring, summer, winter
Places: beach, desert, forest, island, wood

Speaking

Suggested answers:

1 My favourite season is winter. I like the snow and I love snowboarding.

2 There are lots of trees and birds where I live.

3 In my country there are famous lakes and mountains. People like visiting them.

4 Yes, it's important to take care of nature because animals live in nature. It's their home.

Reading

1 B

2 C

3 B

4 C

5 A

Grammar Box

the longest; more famous than

Listening

1 C

2 A

3 D

4 E

5 G

Writing

Sample answer:

Two explorers were lost in the forest. Suddenly, a monkey took their map. After a long time, they arrived at a lovely hotel. They saw the monkey. It was sitting next to the swimming pool eating a banana!

Unit 20 Health, medicine and exercise

Vocabulary

1 1 ambulance
2 clean
3 blood
4 hospital
5 comb
6 sick
7 nurse
8 exercise

You take **medicine** when you are ill.

2 1 hair
    2 eye
    3 back
    4 leg
    5 foot
    6 nose
    7 mouth
    8 arm
    9 stomach

Speaking

Suggested answers:

1 I like swimming and doing yoga. Swimming is fun and yoga helps me to relax.

2 Yes, I prefer doing exercise with other people.

3 I prefer walking because I can walk further. Running makes me tired.

4 Yes, I do. I think it's important to exercise because it's good for your body.

Reading

1 C

2 A

3 C

4 B

5 C

6 B

Listening

1 C

2 B

3 A

Grammar Box

Sample answer: *I'll* go to bed at 9 o'clock.

Writing

Sample answer:

Hi Julie,

I can't come to school today because I feel sick. I fell from the tree in my garden and I hurt my head. I'll lie down and rest at home.

Barbara

Unit 1

Clothes and accessories

belt

blouse

boots

bracelet

cap

earrings

glove

hat

jacket

jeans

raincoat

scarf

shirt

shoes

shorts

skirt

sunglasses

sweater

T-shirt

tie

tights

trainers

umbrella

uniform

wear

Unit 2

Food and drink

apple

barbecue

boiled egg

bottle

bowl

breakfast

café

cafeteria

cheese

chef

chicken

chips

curry

dinner

fish

fork

fridge

glass

jam

kitchen

knife

lunch

meal

meat

menu

orange

pepper

picnic

plate

rice

salad

sandwich

snack

soup

spoon

steak

strawberry

tomato

Unit 3

Colours and time

Colours

black

blue

brown

dark

golden

green

grey

light

orange

pale

pink

purple

red

silver

white

yellow

Time

afternoon

day

midnight

month

morning

noon

spring

tomorrow

winter

yesterday

Unit 4

Family and friends

aunt

brother

children

cousin

daughter

family

friends

grandchildren

granddaughter

grandma

grandparents

grandson

group

guest

husband

married

neighbour

parents

pen friend

sister

son

teenager

uncle

wife

Unit 5

Hobbies and leisure

barbecue

beach

bicycle

camera

camp

camping

campsite

club

cycling

dancing

festival

hobby

holiday

magazine

museum

music

park

party

photograph (photo)

photography

picnic

quiz

reading

restaurant

shops

videogame

Unit 6

House and home

address

apartment

armchair

bathroom

bedroom

bin

blanket

bookcase

curtains

computer

downstairs

drawer

fridge

furniture

garage

garden

home

house

key

kitchen

lamp

lights

living room

office

roof

rubbish

shelf

shower

sink

sofa

toilet

Unit 7

Places: Buildings

bank

bookshop

café

castle

cinema

disco

factory

garage

hospital

hotel

library

modern

museum

old

pharmacy

police station

post office

railway station

school

sports centre

stadium

supermarket

swimming pool

theatre

Unit 8

Sport

badminton

basketball

bat

catch

club

coach

cricket

fishing

hit

hockey

kit

member

practise

riding

rugby

sports centre

surfing

table tennis

team

tennis

throw

volleyball

windsurfing

Unit 9

Documents and texts

bill

book

card

comic

diary

email

form

letter

licence

magazine

menu

message

newspaper

notebook

passport

postcard

project

text

textbook

ticket

Unit 10

Communication and technology

answer

call

camera

chat online

click

computer

download

email

envelope

information

internet

keyboard

laptop

mobile (phone)

mouse

online

password

photograph

photography
printer
screen
surf
tablet
type
video game
website

Unit 11

Education

biology
class
classmate
classroom
desk
diploma
exam
geography
history
homework
lesson
maths
physics
pupil
ruler
science
student
subject
teacher
term
university

Adverbs of frequency

always
never
often
sometimes
usually

Unit 12

Entertainment and media

act
actor
board game
cartoon
chess
classical
concert
dance
dancer
drum
exhibition
festival
guitar
instrument
keyboard
laugh
movie
musician
paint
painter
painting
photograph
photographer

piano
radio
sing
singer
song
television
violin

Unit 13

Personal feelings, opinions and experiences

afraid
alone
angry
bored
busy
clever
difficult
famous
free
happy
hungry
important
interested
lovely
noisy
old
quiet
rich
soft
sorry
strong

tired
well
young

Unit 14

Places: Countryside

area
beach
campsite
farm
field
forest
hill
island
lake
mountains
path
railway
rainforest
river
road
sea
sky
village
wood

Unit 15

Travel and transport

aeroplane
ambulance
boat
car

coach
driver
explorer
helicopter
motorway
mechanic
motorbike
passenger
pilot
platform
roundabout
ship
suitcase
taxi
tour guide
traffic lights
tram
tyre

Unit 16

Work and jobs

artist
businesswoman
cleaner
cook
customer
dentist
desk
doctor
email
farmer
football player
message
office

photographer
police officer
shop
shop assistant
singer
teacher
tennis player
uniform
waiter/waitress
work

Unit 17

Places: Town and city

airport
bridge
bus station
bus stop
car park
city
city centre
corner
market
motorway
park
petrol station
playground
road
roundabout
square
station
town
underground
zoo

Unit 18

Weather and months

Weather

cloudy

cold

foggy

hot

ice

rain

snow

sunny

thunderstorm

weather

windy

Months

January

February

March

April

May

June

July

August

September

October

November

December

Unit 19

The natural world

autumn

bees

camel

desert

east

fire

forest

grass

grow

hill

ice

island

lake

moon

mountain

north

rabbit

sky

south

spring

stars

summer

tree

west

winter

wood

wool

Unit 20

Health, medicine and exercise

ambulance

arm

back

blood

clean

comb

exercise

eye

face

finger

foot

hair

hospital

leg

medicine

mouth

neck

nose

nurse

sick

stomach